Lois Sinclair completed her nursing training in Edinburgh before working in Australia for six months. She then returned to Scotland to marry Colin and start a family. A year in Montreal followed before their growing clan settled in Midlothian where dogs became a part of the household.

Around 2002, Lois left nursing and joined her local veterinary practice as an untrained member of staff.

Through their charity, Gracehounds, she rescued 70 dogs. Lois also has had 14 dogs and 13 cats of her own and enjoys passing on the joy of animals to her three children and six grandchildren.

To Colin, Nick, Jessica, Elliot, their partners
and my six grandchildren.
With Love.

Lois Sinclair

LEARNING FROM ALBI

To Mandie
with Thanks
best wishes
Lois and Albi

AUSTIN MACAULEY PUBLISHERS™

LONDON • CAMBRIDGE • NEW YORK • SHARJAH

A CIP catalogue record for this title is available from the British Library.

ISBN 9781035838363 (Paperback)
ISBN 9781035838387 (ePub e-book)
ISBN 9781035838370 (Audiobook)

www.austinmacauley.com

First Published 2024
Austin Macauley Publishers Ltd®
1 Canada Square
Canary Wharf
London
E14 5AA

Acknowledgements

There are some old friends and some new ones, who have been a part of Albi's story. Now is the time to say thank you.

First, there is Sarah-Jane Le Blanc, who for the last five years has shown me the magic of animals in such a special way. And her husband, Dereck Le Blanc, for his photography skills.

For my friends, Frances, Janet, Eleanor, Pauline, Susie and Lani. You have all played a part in supporting me with practical help, enthusiasm, tears and laughter during the writing of this book.

Martin Jones, Miheala Bodlovic, Pauline Shirlaw, Keith Lomas, Craig Shirlaw, Lindsay Wright, Colin Sinclair, Kerry Stephan and Jo Pagett. Your lovely photographs have helped Albi's story come alive.

Irene Loudon, your written contribution brings to Albi's story another part of his uniqueness.

Christine McVie, I appreciate your research into *The Liberator of Dachau,* a strange and extraordinary twist in Albi's story. The National Library of Scotland, Edinburgh.

ICR Vets, Loanhead, Midlothian. A huge thank you to everyone who has cared for my animals over the years and all the team who continue to care for my dogs. And a big thank you from Albi.

The Royal (Dick) School of Veterinary Studies, the University of Edinburgh, and the Small Animal Hospital, Bush Campus. The care given to Albi and for giving me the opportunity to work with the vet students and teaching staff.

Sonia Rollo, your picture is part of Albi's story.

It is fun swimming at Doggie Paddles, Fife. Thank you, Pauline and Darryl.

Two special places: the people and animals at Borthwick Farm Midlothian. And a smallholding in Midlothian called the Funny Farm where I get to be with donkeys. Thank you, Jo and Jim.

Pauline and Maria at Forever Hounds for bringing Albi into my life. As well as the ever-patient Gwen Matear of Tynewater Dog Training.

Debs Bridges, thank you for introducing me to Sandra.

My editor, Sandra Smith. Your knowledge and expertise have got this story to completion. It has been a wonderful experience working with you.

Table of Contents

How a rescue dog transformed his owner's life before finding his mission to heal and comfort others.

By Lois Sinclair

Foreword

Sarah-Jane Le Blanc, Professional Animal Communicator

There are so many layers to the amazing soul that is Albi: his physical journey, his spiritual journey, as well as his soul's purpose. Lois is equally intuitive and the two of them have formed a bond, enriching each other's lives and sharing thoughts, challenges and experiences that are at the heart of, *'Learning with Albi'.*

It was when Albi underwent his last operation that Lois spotted a poster inviting people to volunteer to work with veterinary students. This turned out to be a catalyst, giving Lois a platform to share years of animal experiences with people who spend their working lives caring for animals. A world of communication.

Lois' big heart and deep love of animals have similarly extended into the equine world. I watched firsthand as she gained the trust of a little pony that hadn't been handled for several years and chose to avoid people. From this unbelievable experience, she has continued to open her heart, responding intuitively to animals while always being guided by them, watching, listening, and noticing.

Albi has played an instrumental role in every step of Lois' journey in discovering her animal communication gifts. I have seen them learn together, grow together, and love together. '*Learning with Albi*' is the culmination of their deep bond. It is a story of friendship and trust, love and wisdom, and will bring a new dimension to the lives of all those who love animals.

Introduction

My family call me the crazy dog lady. No doubt other people do, too. You see, dogs have been a part of my life for as long as I can remember, never failing to fill me with joy. But there's one dog in particular that has changed my life.

In 2015, when I already had five dogs, Albi, a Podenco puppy, came into our home. Almost immediately, we began to develop a love and connection for each other in what would grow into a transformational relationship, one I have decided to share. *Learning from Albi* is the story of a dog who was fostered from Spain, a dog whose dedication, stoicism and bursts of positive energy continually fill me with hope.

I always refer to myself as a pet guardian rather than a pet owner. I do my best for each animal in my care. But I do not own Albi. In fact, he is a free spirit. Albi is highly intelligent and has a sense of humour that draws people to him. To be honest, he is highly intuitive. A few years ago, three of my Greyhounds died within nine months of each other. On each occasion, Albi shared his love with the dying dog, myself and my other dogs, thereby diffusing a distressing situation into something calm and peaceful. This was such a comfort to me. Now, as a Transition Dog, Albi supports people and animals at a time of death, giving comfort to help them as they pass peacefully from this world.

Woven throughout *Learning from Albi* are stories of other dogs, and other animals, that have touched my heart. I also share the importance to me of getting to know Pet Whisperer, Sarah-Jane Le Blanc, who taught me about her world of animal communication – a world where animals talk to us and we can learn how to hear them. Through Sarah-Jane, I have also come to understand the powerful effect on the mind, body and spirit of positive energy, an understanding that has helped me cope with a series of challenges that life has presented over the last few years within my animal and human family.

Another major part of my journey has been managing Albi's health issues, which have led us both to new and unexpected opportunities. His referral from our veterinary practice to an animal hospital for further care and treatment led me to discover a volunteer program working with veterinary students in the area of communication, something Albi and I have done since 2019. Having such a dog has made me aware of the importance of good communication between clients and vets. The health care needs of an animal depend on this. *Learning from Albi* also discusses the subject of euthanasia, including the challenge of saying goodbye to a dearly loved animal and the importance of getting the timing right, how best to support an animal and its owner at such a time, and giving love time and a safe space. These might be topics that the reader finds hard to believe but I have witnessed the power of Albi. Besides, do we have to understand everything?

Learning from Albi is about the wonder of dogs and the incredible relationship that is possible between a human and an animal. Albi has enriched my life in so many ways. Life can be extraordinary when a door is left open to welcome and absorb new experiences. Albi taught me that. Perhaps he can teach you, too?

Chapter 1
I'll Take Him!

All my life I have enjoyed being in the company of animals, with a special place in my heart for dogs. But it took the arrival of Albi, a scruffy, white, deaf Spanish Podenco puppy to enrich my life in so many ways while all the time teaching me with a depth of wisdom – about love, kindness, compassion and empathy – that was way beyond his years.

Albi's first 12 months with us were exhausting and chaotic for everyone but we survived, by which time, he was no longer a foster dog but part of our family. My experience with this exceptional animal, who arrived with more challenges than I had ever encountered before in any dog, led me to write a short book, '*The Love Light in Your Eyes*', about those initial and eventful months. From the moment he came into our garden, I knew that there was something very different and special about him. And I was right. In time, Albi would show me a magical quality, something deeply touching that I had never experienced before.

Albi's story is full of events that some might say are mere coincidences but I believe it was written in the stars that he was going to find his way to us. This was all just meant to be. In fact, before Albi arrived, I had a wondrous sign that he would be coming. One day, while visiting a small art gallery, a picture caught my eye. It was of the oddest-looking dog that I had ever seen, its face seemed more like a cartoon. The image featured a white dog with big eyes, huge ears that stuck out to the sides, an enormous pink nose and appeared to be of no particular breed. The picture entitled, '*The Love Light in Your Eyes*' was by the artist, Sonia Rollo. This quirky painting drew me in, and without hesitation, I knew I had to have it.

The next time I had such a strange and immediate response was four years later when I was sent a photo of Albi. Straight away I said, "I'll take him."

During the previous few years, there had been many changes in my life that would make it possible for Albi and I to eventually meet. Around 2002, I left nursing in the health service to work as an untrained member of staff at a local veterinary practice where I had been a client for many years. This opportunity to work with animals opened the door to everything that was to follow. It was here that I met Bess, a Greyhound brought into the practice, having broken her leg on the racing track. She was an inpatient for eight weeks while, her leg healed and then came home with me. After a few years, I would change direction again.

Through Bess, my introduction to Greyhounds and the difficulties they face led to me to setting up and running a Greyhound rehoming charity. Gracehounds was based at our home where I enjoyed the support of Colin, my husband, and close friend, Pauline Shirlaw, as well as a group of dedicated volunteers who helped with dog walking and fundraising events. This continued for six years and was one of the most rewarding periods of my life. In this short space of time, over 70 dogs came through our home. The anticipation of each new dog arriving, with its individual personalities, past experiences and whatever needs were required, was my challenge – to help each one adapt to a new way of living.

Closing the charity was a hard and sad decision, but a necessary one, as work like this takes over your life. My husband also had a busy job in the NHS and, with the never-ending demands of the charity, the time came when we had to take stock of our own lives. Back then there were five dogs in our home, all having arrived through the charity over the previous few years. They were Ricky, Tabitha, Marcus and Pippa, also Milly our Lurcher who came from Spain via the same route that would, in time, bring Albi to us.

Two years on, life was settled and enjoyable, with time to spend with our dogs and grandchildren who were arriving in rapid succession! Then the photo of Albi appeared out of the blue. My paramedic friend, Pauline, who rescues dogs from Spain, had heard, via social media, about the plight of a Podenco puppy that had been run over in the street. This pup was a stray and required urgent veterinary care; his broken back leg needed to be pinned and plated. What prompted Pauline to send me that picture, I do not know, otherwise, I would have never seen it as I am not a user of social media. It also came at a time when I had become aware that the closure of Gracehounds had left me missing the arrival of a new dog that needed help and the challenge of working out what I would do to make it fit, well and happy. After all, it was the whole process of watching the transformation that took place in front of my eyes that gave me so much joy.

In advance of Albi's arrival, indeed before I had seen his picture, many kind people had rallied to raise sufficient funds to cover his surgery. Several years later, I was to meet one of those people while walking my dogs in a country park near where we live. A girl came running over to us and asked if this was Albi. She had recognised him because of the photos she'd seen and she had read his story. This person had donated money when she had seen the request for help. It was so lovely to be able to thank one of the many generous people who had cared enough to contribute to helping a young dog in distress.

Looking at the photo, I phoned Pauline and said, "If you can get him here, I will foster him." Just like the picture four years before, I had to say, "Yes."

Waiting for Albi's arrival was a lesson in patience! There were days when I wondered whether he'd ever make it. Then, three months after agreeing to offer him a foster home, he arrived.

But it wasn't all good news.

Only at this point was I told that he was deaf. I was a little taken aback but as I already had experience with a blind cat called Alfie as well as Pippa, a three-legged Greyhound, I felt that, together, Albi and I would learn how to cope. By the way, many years ago, when Alfie the cat was alive, I tried several times to write a short story about him and never got very far, so I am now delighted for him to find his place in Albi's story. It would have been fascinating to have had blind Alfie and deaf Albi in my life at the same time, and amazing is the correct word to describe them both.

Bess – Lois Sinclair

Albi – Lois Sinclair

The love light in your eyes by artist Sonia Rollo – Lois Sinclair

Chapter 2
A Giant in the World of Felines

I have had many cats over the years. Although living with a cat is a different relationship to a dog, the bond can be just as strong.

In fact, I was to learn that little Alfie was in a league of his own.

A small white fluffy cat with just a bit of black on his markings, at around six years of age, Alfie found himself in a rescue centre. Several times a week, a member of staff would arrive at the vets where I was working, with a bundle of cat baskets filled with all sizes and colours of cats requiring health checks. One particular morning, I went into one of the consulting rooms to meet that day's furry clients. I took time to hear their individual stories. But there was one little cat sitting on the floor looking up at me. This was Alfie. I was told that nobody would want him as he was blind. Those big eyes facing me had no sight. His plight touched me and I immediately said that he would be coming home with me.

Alfie was to be the most affectionate, loving, calm and fearless cat that I had ever known. He settled in straight away. Our four dogs gave him instant respect. He found his way around the house so fast that you would have thought that he had been here before, navigating up the kitchen chairs, onto the table and settling himself on the blanket which lay over the wall radiator. This was to be his favourite place.

When Alfie spoke to me, it was a loud PRTT, PRTT, PRTT sound if he was looking for me or if I called him. On finding each other, I would bend down and pick him up under his front legs. Our faces would touch then, cradling and holding him close, he would wind his paws round my neck. I loved that and so did he. We often walked around the garden entwined like this, Alfie's head turned back over my shoulder as he sniffed the air. Our garden is big and Alfie loved being out but I had to keep a watchful eye on him. He was quite the escape artist and could be up trees and scaling eight-foot walls with no problem at all. This little creature had acquired resilience and confidence by the bucket load, or, had he just been born like that?

While our home was being renovated, one of the team arrived late afternoon for a meeting. Being distracted, I forgot to bring Alfie into the house with me. Two hours passed before, and to my horror, I remembered that he was still outside. Colin and I rushed outside to look for him. He was nowhere to be found. We searched everywhere, in the garden, down the drive and on the street. I was beside myself with worry because I knew that somehow, he had got out. But where had he gone?

Later that evening, when I feared he was lost forever, the phone rang. Did I have a small blind cat? I did indeed. He had been spotted sitting in the kind lady's garden, her dog standing looking at Alfie, wondering what to make of him. Alfie wore a collar with our details including the fact that he was blind. This cat had walked the whole length of our garden, climbed the wall, and negotiated a six-foot drop into the garden below us. He then continued to head down our neighbour's drive, out of their gate, crossing a busy road before proceeding to walk along the pavement, eventually turning right and into his rescuer's garden. Let me remind you that he was blind!

Thinking back and remembering Alfie's big adventure, I still feel the huge loss that I experienced thinking that he was gone forever and the joy as I ran the whole way to collect him. On seeing him I just said, "Alfie!"

Sitting there looking up, waiting to be hugged, he responded, "PRTT, PRTT, PRTT."

After all these years since he died, I can still sense the softness of his fur and the skinny little body underneath. He was a small cat but with a big personality, such a strong character, and I can still picture him striding about the garden without care.

Alfie was a giant in the world of felines, an extraordinary cat. But now back to Albi.

Alfie and Lois – Colin Sinclair

Chapter 3
From Foster Care to
Permanent Home

From the moment of Albi's arrival, this waif of a dog did not stop running. In fact, his endless energy continued for three months. Colin and I had absolutely no idea what was ahead, which was fortunate. What saved us all – my other dogs included – was that when Albi crashed out, he slept for hours. Then, the minute he woke, the damage and mess started all over again. Dog beds would be dragged out to the garden, and then their insides would be on the outside. Toilet paper, phones, shoes, dog coats, blankets and dog toys were all dismantled. Dog owners understand normal puppy messes but, believe me, this was way beyond normal. It was relentless! The chaos went on daily for months.

The training was a challenge as Albi could not hear instructions and had no eye contact, which is not unusual for a dog brought up on the streets. Also, he was totally uninterested in treats. I tried to work with hand signals but Albi seemed to live in a world of his own and it was hard to get his attention. Not surprisingly, progress was slow. But sometimes you have to just learn to be patient. In time, we were to meet Sarah-Jane, the pet whisperer, who asked Albi why he would never let himself be caught when it came to loading everybody into the van to go for our walk. Albi said, "Walks mean leads and I love to run free." On hearing this, I understood why our large garden suited him so well. Yet, in amongst the frenetic activity, when I looked into Albi's eyes there was something deep and calming in the depth of his soul. I just wanted to understand him. But I had to wait.

I have mentioned Albi at times, appeared to be in his own world and he did seem detached from what was going on around him. However, as the racing about slowed and the general destruction of anything he could get his paws on (thankfully) lessened, he became more connected with us and his lovely personality began to shine. Throughout all of this process, my five dogs treated him with kindness, never getting impatient with Albi and managing (unlike Colin and I!) to ignore much of the goings on.

Albi was our foster dog which meant he was never meant to stay with us permanently. In fact, he got the opportunity to go to what we hoped would be his forever home but he did not settle and was becoming unhappy. Which is why, a few weeks later, I went to collect him.

This time he would stay with us.

Albi and his mess – Lois Sinclair

Chapter 4
Visiting Rights

When fostering, why do some dogs move on and others stay? Honestly, I do not know. There was one dog who arrived and then moved on to her new home, but our bond is still as strong as ever even after all the years that have passed. So, I would like to tell you about Sara Jane the Lurcher.

Living in the Scottish Borders is a magnificent, short-coated and very strong Lurcher called Sara Jane who, at the time of writing, will be ten years old. I think about her often and my heart sings. One day my paramedic friend Pauline, driving past in her ambulance, noticed a small puppy being dragged harshly along a street in Edinburgh at the end of a lead. The person at the other end was hoping to find a buyer for her. Pauline was unable to intervene at the time as she was working but later that day contacted me. The next day, having pooled our resources, she went back to find the pup. That is how Sara Jane found her way to my Greyhound rescue.

In time, she went to her new home and a happy home it was. Then, through nobody's fault, the situation changed. Sara Jane was a sweet-natured dog and had done nothing wrong but had developed into a big powerful animal. Having outgrown her home, it was decided, by all, that it was best she be moved. Thinking back, the tears well up in my eyes remembering her distress at not understanding why she had to leave her home, the distress of her family having to let her go and of course, my distress because I had homed her.

I phoned some friends who have a soft spot for Lurchers and asked if it was possible for Sara Jane to stay with them for a while as a foster dog. Their response to my request was immediate and generous. Kind Keith and Nina said they would give her a home and adopt her. That is how Sara Jane came to be in her forever home with Sam and Archie, two wonderful Lurchers who were already living the dream. They welcomed Sara Jane as if they had been waiting for her their whole lives. All three bonded immediately. What a team!

How do I explain the welcome I receive when I visit? Well, as I arrive at the garden gate, my glasses are placed safely in my pocket, then, as I go through the kitchen door, I have to press my body against the wall to keep my balance as Sara Jane launches herself at me. One day, her family suggested that I watch YouTube videos of loyal dogs welcoming their owners back from military service or some other long absence. They wanted me to see that this is how Sara Jane greets me, with absolute exuberance, thrill and joy written all over her face, her body in perpetual motion. Once the excitement subsides, we collapse together on the sofa and for the rest of the visit, she sits quietly and peacefully with my arms wrapped around her.

When it is time to leave, Sara Jane walks me to the door, before retiring to the sitting room window from where she watches me drive away. She is not sad or unhappy that I have left; this is just how things are. She is where she belongs with her family and I will always visit. I am told that nobody ever gets the greeting that I do, in fact, nothing like it!

I wasn't able to keep every dog that came into my house however much I would have liked to. Sara Jane and I have been through so much together and I am sure she knows that I have tried to do my best and always cared about what happened to her. She understands, I can see it in her eyes.

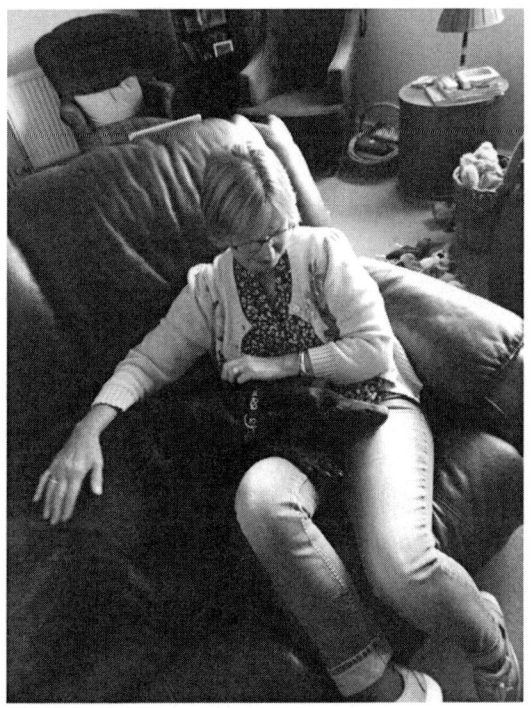

Sara Jane and Lois – Keith Lomas

Chapter 5
Shadow Chasing

I was so pleased to have Albi back, having fallen in love with this quirky dog. But life can take some very strange turns. Two weeks after Albi left, Ricky died. Ricky was eleven and his heart was struggling, so it was time to put him to sleep. He was the most beautiful red Greyhound and had come to me several years earlier as a depressed ex-racing dog, becoming such a lovely, loyal companion. In our loss, the sadness was terrible and the house so empty. I can honestly say if Ricky had died two weeks earlier, Albi would have never left.

Having Albi back was wonderful. Yet he was not the same dog that had left us, having lost his spark. In fact, he looked dejected and in his unhappiness he had begun shadow chasing, which is a behaviour that can be triggered by anxiety and stress, causing dogs to become obsessed with light and shadows, on the move most of the time with little interest in anything else. For years, I carried the guilt that by sending him away, I had caused this, but later when I knew Sarah-Jane, I spoke to her about it. She advised me to let it go, this was all part of Albi's story. Now, I like to think this is correct, everything that has happened makes him so extraordinary. Without these events, there would be no story.

Sadly, having lost Ricky two weeks after Albi went to his new home, we would then also lose Tabitha a fortnight after Albi came back to us. She went to the vet for a routine procedure and did not wake up from the anaesthetic. In the space of two months, we had lost two of our wonderful Greyhounds. Colin and I were devastated.

But for now, my focus was on getting the old Albi back. Shadow chasing was something that I knew nothing about as I had never come across this distressing condition before. I assure you it is awful to watch a dog consumed by obsessional and repetitive patterns of behaviour.

He ran around chasing shadows, climbing walls while uttering a high-pitched screech. In the house, we could close shutters and try our best to keep the light out but outside it was so difficult. Taking Albi for a walk was a nightmare as he bounced on the end of a lead, trying to catch whatever caught his eye.

I was fortunate to have a group of friends who had all been volunteers helping walk our foster dogs when I had Gracehounds and as they had no dogs of their own, they chose to continue walking with me and my dogs. Everyone enjoyed being in the company of the dogs and all called it their weekly dog fix. This was now to prove invaluable help for me, having extra pairs of hands when Albi was testing me to the limit.

He wore a thunder jacket which, for anybody who has not needed to use one on their dog, is a tight-fitting coat that can give the animal a feeling of security and comfort. Albi wore his for weeks. Each day before the back door was opened in the morning, his harness was put on top of his thunder jacket. This made it easier to catch him and, of course, once the lead was attached and the spinning through the air started, it protected his neck from being twisted and pulled around. Writing down these events reminds me so clearly of that time.

Eventually, the screeching stopped, and then there was the day that we went for a walk and Albi behaved like a normal dog. Later, when we returned home and I was sitting on a step in the kitchen, he came over to me, bent down and licked the tip of my nose. Albi had never done that before. Does a day get any better?

It was then suggested to me that Albi might enjoy scent training. This type of training does have the effect of tiring a dog mentally and physically but is a low-impact activity which can help build up a dog's confidence. Scent training gives the opportunity for the dog and owner to create a bond as they work on an activity together and no previous training is required. I thought this might be just the business for Albi and I, so I signed us up for a block of classes which we both enjoyed and it was lovely to see Albi blossom. From there, we continued to do scent training for a while with our teacher but this was on the basis of one-to-one sessions in our garden, which was also helpful.

While all this work was taking place, helping Albi recover and we were adjusting along with Marcus, Milly and Pippa to no longer having Ricky and Tabitha in our lives, along came another Greyhound to join us. This took the number of dogs in my house back up to five.

Ricky – Martin Jones

Tabitha – Martin Jones

Chapter 6
And One More Makes Five

Henry was a beautiful large black Greyhound, an older dog when he was adopted, who went to his new home after a lifetime of racing. I met him within days of his arrival. He was friendly and, considering he had lived in kennels for so long, quickly settled in. But he appeared somewhat institutionalised and, probably due to lack of stimulus, his personality was subdued. This is not unusual with racing dogs and it is wonderful to watch them blossom over time in a loving home.

Henry's family was an older couple who loved him and gave him all the care and kindness needed to make a dog happy. I visited often and he always joined me on the sofa. In time, I introduced him to my four dogs. Henry soon became a fit and healthy dog who wanted to be out and about making friends with other dogs and he thoroughly enjoyed his walks. Sadly, though, his owners' health began to limit their ability to give Henry the companionship and exercise that he needed. I offered to collect him several mornings a week in my van and take him walking with my dogs. Henry loved it! He would jump into my van, settle down with everybody, no problem, and off we would go. This routine continued for several months until his owners told me that he had taken to spending a lot of time standing at the gate looking for me. He had become unsettled. That had not been my intention in solving one problem, yet I had unwittingly created another. Finally, we had to address the issue of Henry's happiness. I had been friends with his family for many years and although it wasn't an easy conversation, we all agreed that Henry's welfare was now the priority. The outcome was that he should come and live with me and my family.

From the moment Henry walked in, his long black tail never stopped and even though he was a large dog he bounced around with joy. Greyhounds do not have much fur or padding on their tails and it is not unusual for them to get injured. After hours of happily wagging his tail against walls and doors, Henry's tail split sending blood splattering all over my kitchen. This type of injury does not heal well and some vets now choose to amputate most of the tail instead of just the tip. Hence, you may spot Greyhounds with very short tails and, yes, Henry joined that particular club. Still undeterred, he continued to wag what was left with enthusiasm.

This lovely dog was a wonderful addition to our family. Pippa, Marcus, Milly and Albi were so welcoming, there was no settling-in period. I often took him to visit his previous family; they loved to see him and I was happy to have him in my life. He thanked me every day by always staying close to me. Marcus and Henry were my two older dogs and they developed such a kind and gentle friendship, completely at ease in each other's company. Sadly, within 15 months, these lovely old gentlemen would have to be put to sleep within two weeks of each other.

Henry – Lois Sinclair

Chapter 7
Dog Attack!

Having dogs can bring much joy, fun and exercise into a day but sometimes an event can happen out of the blue that is none of these.

I want to take you back a few years to my first sighthound, Max, a Deerhound/Greyhound cross who was a magnificent and aristocratic-looking creature, who all other dogs looked up to. He arrived at the veterinary practice needing a home a month after I began working there. By the time I left a few years later, three cats and four dogs had come home with me, including Max who was to become my pride and joy.

Several years later, when I was running Gracehounds, in bounced Marcus, a big Greyhound who was two years old and had not made the grade as a racer. What he lacked in racing ability he made up for in enthusiasm and energy; he was both boisterous and joyful but with kindness in abundance. It soon became clear that he would be staying with us forever. When Max died at 12 years old, he left big boots to fill and Marcus stepped into them with ease. He had, over time, become a serene and thoughtful dog, having long since left his wild days behind him. He was to become my pride and joy, Mark II.

Around the time that Marcus was nine years old, due to a sore foot which was being rested, I would hand him over to Henry's old family while we all went for a walk. They loved to see him and he enjoyed the attention. One morning, I parked the van and went in to collect him. On our way back to the van, I suddenly felt a whoosh of air coming up behind me and had a feeling of impending doom. Two dogs shot past me and went straight to Marcus, one had him by the throat and the other was at his back end, between them they pulled him to the ground. My beautiful big dog hit the pavement without a sound. The noise from the two dogs was horrific and nobody was around even though I was yelling for help. I was afraid that the dog attached to Marcus's throat would kill him, so I waded in to pull it off.

The advice in these situations is to stand back so as not to get hurt but I could not just stand there and watch. I prized open the jaws of the dog but it suddenly turned on me and I felt the most awful pain as it bit deeply into my hand, it then let go to renew its attack on Marcus. By now, a small crowd had gathered; the dog's owner was the last to arrive. Time seemed to stand still as he tried to call his dogs off. In a moment of distraction, Marcus managed to get to his feet and run off in a panic with me following. Even in his state of shock he could hear me calling and slowed down to let me catch up with him. By this time, a paramedic on a motorbike, an ambulance and my husband had arrived. Colin put Marcus in the van with the other dogs, who were clearly distressed as they had witnessed the whole event unfolding, and took Marcus straight to the vet.

The pain in my hand was excruciating and I was given an injection for pain relief and taken to Accident and Emergency at our nearest hospital. Later, I would be transferred to another hospital which had a plastic surgery unit as my hand needed to be operated on. Little did we know that it would be five days before Marcus and I would see each other again. My wonderful, gentle dog had never shown any aggression to humans or animals in his whole life. That this should have happened to him was tragic. Marcus recovered physically but psychologically was never quite the same again. I too was affected psychologically. A dog attack is no different to any other form of violent physical assault on your person. I realised quite quickly that I was afraid to walk my dogs. Up to that point, it had always been such an enjoyable part of my life. I decided to enlist the help of a dog trainer that I knew to work with me and all my dogs to build our confidence again. It took a while but we got there.

At the time of the incident, the police did not arrive until I had been taken from the scene but visited later once I was home from the hospital. No further action was taken against the owner or the animals involved. I learnt that the whole issue of dog attacks is complicated and certainly needs addressing. I had further meetings with the police, the Scottish Society for the Prevention of Cruelty to Animals and dog wardens from different areas and I discussed the issue with one of the vets at my own practice. Also, I met with local councillors and an MSP, who at that time was working on issues related to the Dangerous Dog Act with the intention of taking the need to reform the Act back to the Scottish Parliament. We discussed many problems that the current legislation failed to address. One very basic issue was that there was no particular funding for the kenneling of dogs that had been removed from their homes, which may be for many months. There is also no funding for any behavioural issues that may need to be addressed. It is, instead, a conversation between the police and the council about who funds the stay that has to be discussed for every single dog needing a kennel space. I learnt a lot and people were generous with their time, helping me understand the complicated and frankly depressing business. The needs of the dog seemed to have gotten lost during the drafting of legislation.

At that time, there appeared to be much work to do with all the agencies involved. For me, understanding the complexities of the situation was part of my healing. Finally, in time, I, with Marcus, Henry, Pippa, Milly and Albi were able to find joy in our walks again and move on with our lives.

Max – Craig Shirlaw

Marcus – Martin Jones

Chapter 8
Talented Truffle Hunter

Doing activities with Albi gave him focus and over time, this helped with the shadow chasing, which started to lessen and no longer dominated his life. Five years on, Albi can still dip in and out of chasing shadows but it is a long time ago now since that initial obsession impaired his natural *joie de vivre*.

For some time, Colin and Milly, our Lurcher, had been enjoying the sport of cani cross together. It has been quite popular for several years and here's how it works. Dog and owner run. The human has a wide belt around their waist, the dog wears a harness and they are attached by a thick elasticised line. Colin had been a runner for many years doing triathlons and marathons, so this was a new challenge. He and Milly were enjoying themselves and we wondered whether Albi would like to join in. He was, in fact, very keen. The first outing was a bit traumatic for everybody as the lines all got tangled but once everything was put in order, they were off.

Just a week before our lives were going to be so changed, Albi and I went on a five-day truffle hunting course. Being deaf, Albi possibly has other senses more developed and I know that smell is very important to him, to such an extent that when a good smell catches his attention his nose drips.

Having such a large nose you cannot fail to notice it – the drip, that is.

I thought that truffle training would be fun for us both, the next step up from scenting. We were going to have five days together from 10 am in the morning until 3 pm without a care in the world in the beautiful surroundings on a country estate near where I live. Thankfully, I was teamed with Gwen Matear of Tynewater Dog Training, the same person that had worked with us on scent training.

So, starting on one lovely morning in April and following prior instructions, we arrived with what looked like an enormous amount of stuff. I seemed to have filled a whole suitcase. The training was meant to be fun and led by lots of treats to help the dogs respond. It was a small group and I felt that we stood out like sore thumbs as everybody else had well-trained Labradors and Spaniels who appeared to respond to commands, whistles or an appropriately thrown ball.

Albi did none of these things. Also, due to Albi's lack of hearing and various health issues, I had not managed to teach him any recall; he had to be walked on a lead or he would have been off. It was obvious from the beginning that we were not going to be the star turn!

The plan was that we practise with scented objects which had to be found in the woods and by the end of the week we were to be let loose to find a real truffle. I enjoyed the time just being outside with Albi, despite not achieving very much and interspersed with many coffee breaks. I seem to remember between the sunshine there was some rain, however, being in Midlothian we were all well prepared.

Every other owner and dog looked as if they knew what they were doing; Albi and I did not give that impression. With the concentration span of a gnat, Albi wandered around sniffing and enjoying the scenery with me at the other end of his lead. He did not bark like other dogs and appeared slightly aloof. He watched but did not interact.

On the last day, we were given real truffles, or should I say one truffle that we had to break into little pieces. These were then hidden at the base of trees and we guided our dogs close and hoped that they would sniff the truffle out. After four days of feeling a bit of a failure, Albi and I had cracked it. He found his truffle! I was so proud. We finished our week on a high.

Even though we did not know it at the time, events were about to unfold, which would turn me and my dogs' world upside down and would then lead me to find and contact Sarah-Jane, the pet whisperer for the first time. Later, Albi was to tell her about truffle training, "That I had kept the other dogs calm and had been very good at it, and would like to do it again."

Was he good at keeping the other dogs calm or was it his talent as a truffle hunter that he was talking about? I am not quite sure, but it made me smile.

Albi on his truffle training – Lois Sinclair

Chapter 9
Knowing When to Say Goodbye

When I was working at the vet's practice, I witnessed something that had a profound effect on me. A client brought in his beloved old Collie to be put to sleep. After this was done, the dog was laid on a blanket in a kennel, the client then went out to his car and brought in a young Collie. The puppy went into the kennel and stood beside his old friend; he took a big sniff and then walked off with his owner. That little dog had said goodbye, never to be left wondering what had happened to his friend and companion. Since that day, all my dogs are put to sleep at home with their friends beside them, the only exception being Tabitha who died unexpectedly as I have already mentioned when having minor surgery. For her, we were all in shock, but I knew what I had to do. So, I put my other four dogs in the car, drove to the practice, and we all went in to say goodbye to Tabitha. Dogs can be left heartbroken when a companion dies but we would come to see that Albi knew instinctively how to comfort the dying and reassure the living.

For every owner, possibly the hardest decision ever to be made is the timing of putting to sleep a dearly loved pet. Within ten months, I found myself in that situation three times. My sadness and distress at losing first Pippa, followed by Marcus and Henry was terrible but to have Albi present and watch how he behaved on each occasion was the most moving experience, one that gave me comfort. I am also privileged to have witnessed such events.

Pippa was a small, black, feisty Greyhound who was part of our family for seven years. She came to me at two years old with a broken leg having been injured on the racing track. Her owner no longer wanted her. It was immediately obvious that her leg had to be amputated, the damage being irreparable. Pippa lived life to the fullest playing and running with the other dogs, often up front leading the walk. Unfortunately, no matter how fit they are, these dogs appear to have a shorter life span due to the strain put on their remaining three legs. To amputate a leg is just the beginning, but to keep a dog fit, slim and well-exercised lasts their whole lifetime. At times, Pippa would have severe muscle spasms, caused by her back twisting, giving her pain. She would become tired with the effort of keeping up with the other dogs. This saddened her as she was so much part of the group though the others were aware of her struggles. She got through these periods with physiotherapy, acupuncture and pain relief and she always bounced back, but when Pippa was nine, she deteriorated significantly. I knew this time my efforts to help and sustain her were not going to work. The heartbreaking decision to put her to sleep was made easier by the fact that one evening, running around the garden after the other dogs, her remaining back leg suddenly dipped down, the power seeming to go out of it in slow motion. Watching this made up my mind. The following morning, before the vet arrived, Pippa walked out onto our verandah, climbed up on the sofa and lay down. I sat with her and the other dogs were close by as we waited together for the vet. When he joined us, Pippa welcomed him but did not move. It was the same vet who had amputated her leg seven years previously. It seemed so right that he should be with Pippa at the end.

Pippa was at peace knowing this was her time. As she was slipping away, Albi moved forward and quietly stood over her, then, as she took her last breath, he turned looking up at me. I gasped, because of the look in his eyes; I could see into his soul, this strange and wonderful dog. I felt as though time stood still. I had never seen anything quite like it. Albi moved away as she was laid on a blanket, then came forward again, bent down and licked her.

There was a lovely sense of peace and comfort all around us.

It is now nine months since Pippa was put to sleep. Marcus, by this time, was nearly eleven years old and had begun to slow down. His back legs and lower back were causing him problems, though he soldiered on, never complaining, and always on hand to welcome visitors into our home. Marcus was such a kind dog; he and I just loved each other, it was as simple as that.

I knew that the day was drawing near and that I would have to let him go but dogs can tell you when it is time and Marcus did. One morning, the two of us were slowly walking along our street and he just stopped. I said quietly to him, "Would you like to go home?" He turned around and we headed back. The next morning, while we waited for the vet to arrive, Marcus climbed onto the same sofa that little Pippa had chosen a few months before. I sat down beside him and we waited. When the vet, who had known him all the years he had been with me arrived, Marcus got up and walked to the gate as he always did and escorted her in where he returned to the sofa, lay down and waited. Like Pippa, Marcus knew that it was his time. With me beside him, as he was slipping away, Albi came over to join us, and once he took his last breath, Albi then lent forward and licked him. Albi exudes an inner peace and understanding that has the effect of bringing a sense of calm to those around him. It was beautiful to watch.

A few days later, Henry had X-rays taken of his neck and spine as he had taken to walking with his head down and panting. The X-rays showed an area of pressure on his neck pressing on his spinal cord; this was causing him serious pain. What a brave uncomplaining dog Henry had been. We had not had him for very long but he had given us so much love and it had been a joy to have had him in our lives. Henry was now about ten and if any intervention was possible, it would have been too traumatic for him. It was a mere two weeks since Marcus had been put to sleep; now it was Henry's time.

The place where he loved to be was the back of my van with the doors open so that the sun could stream in, bathing him in warmth and light as, at the same time, he could keep an eye on what was going on in his garden. This is where Henry would be put to sleep. The vet who came that day was the proud owner of two Greyhounds and was well aware that I was about to put to sleep my last Greyhound and already feeling a sense of impending loss. Henry was in his special place with me beside him as she climbed into the van to join us. As if aware of what was happening, Albi then jumped into the van and lay down beside me. Then the wonderful sense of calm and peace that I had felt twice before filled the van.

Afterwards, I would remember how Albi shared his kindness and love with each dog as they passed from life to death.

Euthanasia is an emotional subject and one I will come back to later in the book but here I just want the reader to feel the power of Albi and how he behaved. I am sure there will be other people who have maybe witnessed a similar event with one of their dogs and the impact that it has had on them. Over the years, I had grown to believe in the importance of a *good* end-of-life parting between owner and animal companion. Then Albi came into my life and showed me what he could do. This has cemented my belief.

To have a dog like Albi in my life is to be blessed.

Pippa and Albi – Lois Sinclair

Marcus and Henry – Lois Sinclair

Chapter 10
Transition Dog

Around the time Pippa was put to sleep, suddenly, out of the blue, Albi appeared to be in terrible pain. It was the back leg that had been pinned and plated when he was a puppy in Spain, and since then it had stood out at a slight angle. The vet had taken X-rays, yet everything appeared to be in the correct place and looked fine. I took him home with pain relief and was to give him a week of rest. Things settled and life went back to normal. We could not have imagined what was ahead for Albi.

Six months later, at the time of putting Marcus and Henry to sleep, the pain in Albi's leg returned. This time I knew that something was very wrong. Albi was to have the most horrendous next few months and there were times that I thought I might lose him. It was decided that major surgery was required to remove the pins and plate from his leg. Unfortunately, during the operation, the last pin was found to be so deeply embedded that removal was not possible. Instead, it was agreed that that final pin had to be left in place. It was hoped at this point that Albi would make a good recovery.

This was in the summer of 2018 and there were going to be several more challenges ahead.

A year previously, my husband, Colin had been diagnosed with a progressive neurological condition and, following a deterioration in his health, he was admitted to the hospital. It would be another 16 months before we would have a definitive diagnosis. Colin was not going to be at home when I had to make the decision to put Marcus to sleep, followed closely afterwards by Henry.

All these events had a terrible effect on Milly who was devastated. She had lost her three Greyhound companions within nine months, Colin was in the hospital, and Albi had had the first of what was to be four operations in all. Her sadness was palpable and I could see the misery in her eyes. It felt to me that Milly and I were the last two standing; how could I help her? Over the years, I have tried different ways to comfort a distressed animal always treating each one as an individual, and not using the one size fits all approach. I had read about the work of pet whisperers in the past and though I had no first-hand experience myself, I had always been interested in their work. I decided that this was the time to find one such person and see where it would take us.

It is always exciting to try a completely new approach to a problem. Someone I knew, gave me Sarah-Jane Le Blanc's name and I looked up her website. I do like to speak to people where possible, rather than email so I phoned Sarah-Jane. Immediately, I was drawn to her warmth and intrigued to find out what this pet whispering was all about. It is now three years since that call and I have learnt so much about the fascinating world of animal communication and how body energy can have such an impact on healing, the mind, body and spirit, for animals and humans.

I booked two separate sessions that were conducted long distance with Sarah-Jane working from photographs that I had sent of Milly and Albi. After each session, there was a phone call during which Sarah-Jane shared all the information each dog had given to her. I was in no doubt about the conversations between them, they sounded like my dogs and their individual personalities. What they talked about was extraordinary along with the depth of feeling from each of them.

Albi and Milly both shared with Sarah-Jane that they were aware of Colin's deteriorating health.

Milly came across as a dog affected by all the change and losses over the last year, she was sad and fearful for the future. She was afraid that Albi might die. She was worried about Dad (Colin) and wanted him to be out walking through the woods with her and Albi. She knows that nature is healing but is also aware that Dad does not think the same way. Milly mentioned rose-tinted specs as a positive way of coping and this helped me understand life from Colin's perspective, which was helpful. Milly also needed reassurance that she was in her forever home.

Everything that Milly shared was a normal reaction to the uncertainty going on around her. Sarah-Jane would provide the healing through energy work along with constant reassurance from me that she would be with me always. Even though she has been part of our family for many years, the little stray dog in her has never quite believed that she belongs here with us in our home.

Then came the call to follow up on what Albi had shared with Sarah-Jane.

Here are some extracts from the notes that Sarah-Jane took at the time of communicating with Albi: "All the animals that I communicate with are special. They are unique and individual and will always have their own place in my heart. However, every so often, one exceptional soul comes along that stirs a different part of my heart. A deeper part, leaving me forever touched in a unique and extraordinary way. Albi was one such soul. I was blown away by the depth of his essence, the vastness of his soul, with wisdom way beyond his chronological years, deep, deep unconditional love, patience, forgiveness, understanding and loyalty. This young lad was an old soul with a huge heart and was here to teach. Despite all that this boy had – was continuing – to endure, physically, he had a happy heart, a forgiving nature and a deep desire to help all those who were helping him."

There were several things that Albi told Sarah-Jane that day, but the one thing I will mention at this point is that Albi is a Transition Dog, a dog that is here to help others pass over to the other side. He said, "It has been a really tough time for everyone – especially Mum (me) and Milly. Yet I have a different approach. I am able to see it for what it is. Of course, it is always sad to lose loved ones, yet the joy in being with them as they leave this world and knowing you are giving them strength to make the journey to the next world, that makes it all okay. And do you know what, Sarah-Jane? They will be okay. I trust that."

I have seen with my own eyes while watching Pippa, Marcus and Henry slip away, how Albi behaved at the time of each event, the incredible calm and peace that seemed to embrace us all and give such comfort.

There was a question that I had asked Sarah-Jane to put to Albi. I wanted her to tell him about the next operation that he was about to have. I need not have been concerned; he knew already. No surprise there! He said that he could see everyone was talking about him. And he asked, "Can I have a small tasty snack before fasting begins, a nice slice of roast beef would fit the bill, grand!" To my knowledge, Albi had never had roast beef before but from then on, he got some before each operation as requested.

At the end of their session, Albi finished with something that touched Sarah-Jane deeply. He said, "I always prayed that my forever home would be with Mum," and he is so grateful for that wish to have come true.

Chapter 11
Surgery and the Road
to Recovery

Over the summer of 2018, Albi was to have a further two operations on his leg caused by complications from the initial surgery. He just did not seem to be getting better. What was going on? Repeat bloods were taken at the vets and the results this time showed that something was amiss. It was decided that the time had come to get an appointment at the referral hospital to see an orthopaedic specialist. The appointment came through quickly, we only had to wait a week. Unfortunately, Albi couldn't wait.

One morning, I awoke early and went downstairs to see how he was. He was lying in his bed and looked miserable or, to be more accurate, broken after so many months of keeping going when his lovely personality had continued to shine through. I could never have given up on him as he had never given up but on this particular day, he looked as if he had just had enough. His eyes were dull with pain and his beautiful, thick white fur looked like an overcoat that was far too big for him.

I put him in the car, drove to the vet, and we sat and waited for them to open. Luckily for us, it was the same vet that had taken the last blood sample and had been involved in the discussion to send off the referral. Fortunately, we knew each other well. Taking a look at us both, she said, "I am going to do two things, bring you a cup of tea and make a call to the referral hospital to ask if Albi's appointment can be brought forward." Albi and I were left in the consulting room, both sitting on the floor and me weeping into a cup of tea. It takes time to be kind and I was so grateful that morning for the vet's empathy and compassion.

Within two hours, Albi and I were seen at the referral hospital. On looking at Albi, the orthopaedic vet quickly decided not to put him through any more physical examinations, as he was extremely sore. The X-rays sent from my practice were clearly not showing any problems, they did not need to be repeated, instead, Albi was to go straight for a CT scan.

Meanwhile, I went home to wait.

A few hours went by and finally, the phone rang. The results were a shock to everybody who knew Albi.

Apparently, around the time Albi had been in a road traffic accident and had undergone surgery in Spain to repair his broken leg, the infection had been introduced causing two holes deep inside his femur and hidden beneath the plate, which could not be seen on X-rays. As a result, Albi had osteomyelitis. Bone pain is dreadful and this amazing dog had endured this situation, getting worse over a period of four years. Later that day, I went back to collect Albi and discuss the plan with the vet for his care and treatment. The date was set for surgery to remove the final pin, the one that was causing the problem, but I was warned that the bone could fracture under the pressure that would be needed to get it out. If this happened, Albi's leg would have to be amputated. There was no choice, the operation was essential. Nevertheless, I was most concerned because Albi had been coping with infection for a long time and he was now not well. I was afraid that he might die.

The night before surgery, two friends offered to come to the house to bathe Albi: Marie, who has a dog grooming business, and her partner Pauline, who brought Albi into my life. They arrived with all their paraphernalia. Gently popping Albi in the bath, he was given a good wash, and then wrapped up in a warm towel, followed by a blow dry. By the end, he looked like a big Mr Fluff monster. We just hoped that by doing our best for him, this would raise the odds for a successful outcome.

The following morning, while I was driving Albi to the dog hospital and he was being accompanied by one of his large teddy bears, I got to thinking about this incredible love of big soft toys that he had developed, when had it happened and why were they so important to him?

In the chaotic early days, he was so busy dismantling anything that he found, soft toys suffered the same fate as everything else. Possibly they became a comforting thing around the time that the pain in his leg increased. These were not small toys but huge teddy bears. They were carried around the garden; when he was sleeping, he was usually lying or resting his head on one. There were up to a dozen at any one time spread around the house, garden or in my van, looking as if there had been a massacre with bodies everywhere. It always seemed incongruous, seeing this large white dog cuddled up to a teddy. In fact, if the bear happened to be white, it was difficult to see where Albi started and the bear ended. He will often pick up a teddy on our way out of the gate and proudly marches along the street, head held high with a bear hanging from his mouth. He looks so funny – quite ridiculous, in fact – but it makes people smile. It is Albi spreading happiness and joy around, it is what he is here for, so he has told Sarah-Jane.

Whenever Albi went for surgery, a bear went too. On one occasion, I was waiting in the practice car park for Albi to be brought out to me. A tall vet who has a penchant for hats, approached with said hat firmly in place, one hand holding a lead with Albi attached to the other end and under his other arm one of Albi's super-sized teddy bears with a bright red ribbon tied in a bow around his neck. It was a sight to behold and my face broke into a huge grin. This vet was doing his care in the community; nothing was too much trouble for his patient.

Once the bears become soggy, scruffy and bits are hanging out, I take a trip to the local charity shop to replenish our stock. On my return home, Albi greets me with a broad smile and is in seventh heaven as he inspects the new selection of bears and their variety of sizes depending on what is available. In time, when Alice came into our lives, she and Albi would have great fun racing around the garden, this skinny black Greyhound and a large, white fluffy Podenco running side by side sharing a huge teddy between their teeth.

During the drive to the hospital, I thought of all that he and I had been through together. This funny clown of a dog, who was so incredibly deep, stoical and strong. I had always known he was an old soul inside a young dog's body. These thoughts whirled around in my head then, before I knew it, I was handing Albi over to the vet and he was taken away to be prepared for surgery. It was going to be a long morning waiting for the phone call to tell me how everything had gone and how Albi was. Would he be missing a leg?

The operating theatre was packed, the vet doing Albi's surgery that morning was keen to get started and up for the challenge to remove the pin without fracturing the femur. It was shared with me afterwards that there was a bit of breath-holding going on among the spectators. This was going to be difficult and nobody could accurately anticipate the outcome. I have no idea how long it took to remove the deeply embedded pin but there was a sense of communal relief when it appeared and no further damage caused. A brilliant result.

I was to hear later that back at my practice, there were many people working that morning who were thinking about Albi and keeping their fingers crossed for him. I am grateful to everybody who has been involved in Albi's care, at the referral hospital and my own vet's practice. Care for Albi and kindness to both of us.

However, we were not yet out of the woods. Albi had been prescribed a variety of antibiotics for months due to being treated for various infections, so the vet did not want to prescribe any more until the laboratory had discovered what the particular infection was that had caused the osteomyelitis. Three days after surgery, when I went to collect Albi to bring him home, he looked fairly ropy and was on pain relief but he still had an untreated infection. His stay at home did not last long as by tea-time we were on our way back to the hospital; he really was not well and I felt that it would be better for him to be readmitted so that the staff could keep him sedated until the antibiotic treatment began. In all, he would be there another five days. Finally, the results that we were waiting for came back and antibiotic treatment began.

Albi, the amazing Podenco, was finally coming home and beginning the road to recovery.

Albi recovering from his second operation with
Milly – Lois Sinclair

Albi and one of his bears going visiting friends
– Lois Sinclair

Chapter 12
Time for a Swim

The first six weeks at home were very quiet for Albi as he had to live in a crate and was only allowed out to go to the toilet in order to give his leg time to rest after all the trauma of removing that last obstinate pin. He was a good patient and did a lot of sleeping which gave his body time to heal. Then we moved slowly on to building up exercise, along with the help of physiotherapy. Gradually, he started to look better every day.

Then I heard about a place called Doggie Paddles in Fife where I could take him swimming. Having used hydrotherapy before for Pippa when she had had her leg amputated and knowing how much she enjoyed it, I hoped that Albi might feel the same way. Previously, I had used a pool nearer home where Pippa had been lowered into the water by a hoist before swimming up and down on the end of a pole. This approach had been fine for her but I knew this would not appeal to Albi.

So off to Fife we went once a week. The owners are kind people who love working with dogs but on our arrival on the first day Albi, having been lifted into the water by Darryl and handed over to his partner Pauline (the third and final Pauline in this book) who was waiting to take over, was not quite as brave as usual. Given half a chance Albi would have propelled himself out of the water and out of the door at great speed. However, we quickly realised that he was more confident with Darryl who had by now climbed into the water to join them. From then on, it was to be Darryl and Albi, much to Pauline's disappointment though Albi did allow Pauline to do his shower, shampoo, big towel rub and blow dry, which he always enjoyed at the end. I got to choose which glorious dog perfume was to be applied and he left the building smelling heavenly.

Albi always gave Pauline his undivided attention and a special lick, which I can honestly say he does not hand out often. This is Albi's way, perhaps, for making up, as she is not his chosen swimming companion. After we went there a few times, I was asked if I would like to join them in the water. To be swimming along beside Albi is such a lovely thing to share together, he is a beautiful swimmer and gently glides up and down the pool.

Then, in April 2019, Alice came into our lives. I had promised myself that once Albi was well, I would get another Greyhound because the house felt as though something was missing. When she had begun to settle with us and was about five months old, I asked if she could join us in the pool. In my past experience with Greyhounds, I had never known one who enjoyed the water except Pippa doing her hydrotherapy sessions. I wondered if introducing Alice as a puppy would make a difference. It certainly did, she loved it immediately and would hurtle up and down the pool as fast as she could go to catch the toys that were being thrown for her. Although graceful on land, she was not a creature of grace in the water, creating much splashing as Albi cruised up and down, going at his own dignified pace.

Apart from being good for Albi, we all enjoyed our time in the water together. Albi shared his thoughts on swimming with Sarah-Jane which are, "He prefers to swim by himself but if it helps Mum, he will share the pool with Alice."

Much later, we were to go through a period of time when Covid had us in lockdown and we could not swim. It was very interesting, because, when we returned to Doggie Paddles, there were two distinct changes. Albi went straight into the water to join Pauline, much to her delight. For whatever reason best known to himself, he had decided that it was now fine to swim with her. Alice, on the other hand, had forgotten about being in the water previously and was afraid. It took a little bit of time to settle her in, then whoosh, she was off, and loving it again. The simplest pleasures can be such fun.

Dogs never fail to surprise us.

Albi enjoying his swimming – Pauline Shirlaw

Chapter 13
Star Pupil

Sarah-Jane organises weekend workshops, during which, with a small group of interested participants, she shares her skill of animal communication and teaches others how they may develop their own skills in order to do the same.

In October 2018, with a weekend booked for training, Sarah-Jane asked me if I would drive Albi to Fife to be a guest dog for a group of students to work with. That afternoon was to be fascinating for me, I was there as Albi's chauffeur and not expected to say or do anything. Other dogs had been invited for the morning session. No details of the dogs would be shared with the group beforehand, the students would, in turn, have to share with everybody what knowledge they had acquired from the dog.

It was amazing the details of Albi that each person had learnt from him. At this stage, he was not at his best, health-wise (we did not know at the time there would be a fourth and final operation a few weeks ahead), but this group of people were bowled over by this extraordinary dog and his powerful presence; they could feel his deep soul and his ability to communicate with them.

There was a lady present that day called Irene, who had come along with friends, she knew Sarah-Jane as she had attended previous workshops. Irene wrote the following for me about her first experience of meeting Albi.

"For the practical session, Sarah-Jane had arranged for some pet owners (guardians as she referred to them) to present their dogs.

"Lovely though they all were, there was one in particular with which I was to have a most remarkable experience. He was a magnificent rescued Spanish Podenco.

"On his arrival in Scotland, he had been initially fostered and subsequently adopted by his loving guardian Lois.

"Throughout the training session I had been happy to be first in the group to share my experience, but not this time. My communication with Albi had been staggering, so much so, that I was concerned how it would be received by the group and in particular, by Albi's guardian. Consequently, I held back to the last but knew I must be bold and share what Albi had told me (telepathically) regardless of what anyone might think of me.

"According to Albi, as a guard dog in a WWII German concentration camp, he had witnessed many deaths at the hands of firing squads. He had chosen to come back to earth to atone for the sins of the perpetrators through the spreading of love.

"To my relief, no-one questioned my sanity. Albi's guardian was very accepting of what I was sharing for she had understood from the outset that Albi is an exceptional dog. It was then that I learned that Albi is deaf so cannot respond to everyday communication but reacts to certain noise vibrations that could be interpreted as ominous sounds from his past.

"When we parted at the end of the day, I knew that our paths would cross again, such had been the impact of this extraordinary dog on me."

It was a memorable afternoon for everyone. I remember the room was buzzing and filled with such positivity which is the effect that Albi has on people and our session ran on for an extra hour, only drawing to a close because of the need to complete other work on the programme.

A few months later, in January 2019, Albi, I and Irene were to meet again. Albi had come through his last operation and was beginning to look well. I was so pleased to be taking him back to visit Sarah-Jane and to let her see him now on the mend. This time the workshop was about healing with energy and the participants were to put their hands over Albi and become aware of areas in his body that had health issues. Again, the results were amazing as each person explained what they felt. Albi, of course, was the star turn and enjoyed meeting everyone. It would be a year before we saw Irene again when she visited me and my dogs at home.

Finally, in February 2020, Irene came to spend the day with Albi and I, also meeting Milly and Alice for the first time. Watching Irene and Albi together is very interesting. They are not all over each other as some people and dogs are when they are happy to see somebody they like. Nevertheless, it is obvious watching Albi and Irene together that they have a deep understanding between them and mutual respect for each other.

One winter's day, we sat by the fire with Albi and Alice. Suddenly, Alice started to behave badly, wanting attention from Albi. This caused Albi to growl making him sound aggressive, something that he is not. I could see that Alice was clearly making him feel uncomfortable, so I put her out of the room. With that, Albi stretched out in front of the fire. Irene told me that he was telling her, "This is sooooo good." A while later, I opened the door and let Alice back in to join us. She absolutely flounced in and stomped over to her sofa.

She told Irene, "It is not fair! Why did I get sent out? Albi is Mum's favourite." It was just like human siblings complaining about each other while discussing the family pecking order.

Later in the day, I asked Irene if Albi had previously shared more details about his past life with her. Indeed, he had. Albi had been a guard dog in a German concentration camp during WWII, his breed was a Doberman. Alex Kershaw has written in his book, *The Liberator of Dachau* in a chapter entitled, *'The Hounds of Hell'* that, "Other than Alsatians and Dobermans, there were Great Danes, Boxers, Shepherds and Wolfhounds. Albi had managed to escape but never found a home and had eventually died of hunger."

What extraordinary information to be given. To believe in reincarnation or not is up to each individual. The voice that Irene senses goes with what I would expect to hear from Albi, a droll, deep voice like that of an older man with a dry sense of humour. Albi also somehow manages to give the impression that he stands to the side of life in a quiet, detached sort of way. That is how I see him but it is always wonderful for me when other people can feel that sense of him.

At one point during our conversation, Irene asked me if I had read the book called, *'A Dog's Purpose'*. Funnily enough, I had just finished reading it before her visit. This book is written by WB Cameron and in a review by the *Library Journal* is described as, "The remarkable story of one endearing dog's search over the course of several lives. More than just another charming dog story. *A Dog's Purpose* touches on the universal quest for an answer to life's most basic question, Why are we here?"

Irene said, "Could the same be said of Albi?" I remember when I was reading the book that the hairs on my neck stood up when suddenly, it struck me that this was a fictional story first told verbally and then put into book form for the author's wife to give comfort after the death of her dog, but here was I with a dog in real life that I had been told had come back for a purpose.

That day, Irene finished our conversation by talking to me about the power of love, distress and sadness, and how these feelings can flow both ways between owners and animals. The story that she shared with me related to when she was training in animal healing. The students were shown a picture of a beautiful dog, in response to which all expressed a feeling of heaviness and sadness. To everyone's surprise, it transpired that the dog had died two years previously. Happily, by the end of the training practice with the shared group, the sensation was that of calmness and resolve. The dog had been healed of its sadness at having witnessed its master's grief.

For me, this story supports my belief that during the time of parting it is so important to support, care and comfort the animal and its owner.

It had been such an interesting day, one which had left me with much to think about, but it was also very joyful and fun. Suddenly, it was over and time to take Irene back to the station. We all piled into the van, dogs included. Before long, there was a sound of moaning coming from the back. I was sure that the problem was Alice but shouted back to Albi, "What is going on?" Irene said from Albi.

"It's Alice, she always makes that noise when she wants attention!"

Kershaw,Alex. The Liberator: One World War II Soldier's 500-day Odyssey from the beaches of Sicily to the Gates of Dachau. 2013. Print.

Cameron,W.Bruce. A Dog's Purpose: A Novel for Humans. 2017. Print.

The review quoted was written by the Library Journal and is at the front of the book.

Chapter 14
Animal Health Care

In the 1980s, Colin, I and our little family, which consisted of three children of five, three, and two years, along with one cat and a newly acquired dog, moved out of Edinburgh to live in Midlothian. Our house was just at the limit of where we could be for Colin to be on call for the hospital. It had been our intention to get a dog as soon as we moved but things do not always go according to plan. One weekend, six weeks before the move, Colin was on call and while in the hospital was approached by a member of staff in tears who was having to find a home for her mother's dog, as she was by now terminally ill. Colin arranged for the dog to be brought to meet us the following evening. On the dot of 7 pm the next day, the doorbell rang and, on opening the door, I saw two people and a dog.

Our children were safely tucked up in bed knowing nothing about the events that were unfolding downstairs. This dog was only nine months old and in this short period of time, life had not been very kind to him. A few months previously, he had been found staked out beside the River Forth so the incoming tide would drown him but he was spotted by a member of this caring family and taken home. He was a large brown and white rough Collie cross, and very hairy. I had been looking forward to finding a Labrador and this did not match up. Colin had sold him to me by saying that he was a Lab/Collie cross. It was obvious that he was definitely not!

Out in the hall, Colin whispered to me that the dog needed a home and we could get a Labrador in the future. It was just as well that he would be staying with us as he had arrived with all his belongings. We renamed him Christopher, who was to be Colin's first dog. There had always been dogs in my family when I was growing up but Colin and Christopher were to develop a strong bond.

We soon realised that Christopher had not had any training and our garden was not as secure as we had thought. Dog training and making the garden Christopher-proof were now a top priority. This dog was to become a wonderful member of our family for the next 16 years. Two years later, I did get my black Labrador puppy, Murphy, and these two dogs were great companions for the rest of their lives.

Thirty-five years later, we are still here, in this lovely house with a large sunny garden surrounded by a high stone wall, with wonderful views over the Pentland Hills and I am still with the same veterinary practice that I registered with on our arrival to the area. At the time of moving here, I did not know what the future held. I knew that I wanted animals in my life but had no idea how one thing would lead to another with dogs and cats that just kept arriving. Even though I only write about our little blind cat, Alfie, there were 13 others that would share their lives with us, as well as all the dogs.

The one thing that the animals would have in common was that they all required veterinary care at regular times in their lives. I have no professional qualifications in animal care, which I have previously mentioned, but I have spent time working at the vet practice, volunteering at a donkey sanctuary, having my own Greyhound rescue and caring for all my own animals. I hope that these learning experiences have given me some understanding of what care is needed to give an animal the best environment in which to thrive. Veterinary care is part of the overall picture.

The importance of the client and vet relationship cannot be underestimated; an animal relies on good communication so that the appropriate and best care can be given where and when needed, as they cannot speak for themselves. It can be bad enough coming out of a GP surgery thinking, *Oh dear, that did not go very well.* Imagine an animal listening to their owner and vet having a conversation and thinking, *Oh dear, this is not going well!*

The subject of communication really started to interest me when Albi came into my life. His needs were so complex, I knew that I would have to have practical help and support from professionals, not just the vets at my practice but also people qualified in other areas of animal care. With this approach, I have met many people from different disciplines who have given me fresh insight that has proved to be helpful when looking after my own animals.

Albi is a dog that people can learn so much from. His health problems have caused him to suffer terribly at times and unfortunately for him, he has not always presented as a textbook case. Yet it is such cases as his that give great opportunities for learning. I have always felt that continuity of care is important but as a practice expands it does make it harder at times though worthwhile as far as possible.

When I first joined the practice as a client, there was one vet. Many years later, when I went to work at the practice there were three vets and by the time I left, this had increased to four. Now, all these years later, the number of vets is in double figures. With so many people working in a busy practice, it can sometimes make it difficult to see a particular person. There is also the volume of clients due to the amount of pet ownership that has taken such a leap forward, especially during Covid. This has now caused some practices to close their doors to new clients. In fact, in some areas of the country there now appears to be a shortage of vets.

The world of health care is becoming a worrying area for those professionals giving care, as well as the patients – human or animal – on the receiving end. It has proved to be so important for Albi to have continuity of care when he was on the mend after the difficult time of operations and infection. I knew there would be long-term problems due to trauma that would have to be managed but I do not think that anybody anticipated the terrible build-up of pain due to muscle spasms, osteoarthritis and nerve pathways being affected caused by chronic pain. Albi would quietly and stoically cope until he could no longer hide all the pain he was feeling. This pattern has happened twice in the last couple of years giving the impression that there may be a further health issue which has obviously led to more investigations.

Chronic pain is hard to manage in humans. But people can at least explain what they are feeling and there are clinics in the health service to treat this difficult and distressing problem. With animals, we have to watch carefully because they try to hide the pain. The second time that Albi's pain levels escalated, I could sense how restless he was at night and fidgeting in the evening. How tired his eyes looked and his usual big white coat seemed to go flat and grey. Even so, this dog was still going on walks, running up and down stairs, and playing with his toys and companions, Milly and Alice.

We now have the full picture and the correct medication, along with the help of physiotherapy, using a water treadmill and laser treatment, and energy work by Sarah-Jane. Unfortunately, we stopped Albi's acupuncture after three weeks because he could not settle into it which was disappointing as I had seen with Pippa and Marcus how effective it can be, but animals, just like people, are all different and it is about finding the best way to help an individual. All this treatment has made a huge difference to Albi. He was by now looking well again. Working out the care needs of a dog like Albi is not possible unless the whole picture is discussed and taken into consideration. I am grateful to everybody involved in his ongoing care.

For anybody who has an animal in their lives, they know this can come at a financial cost, even if the animal has insurance. There may be people reading this who have gone the extra mile for their pets because they felt that they just had to keep going even though the bills were mounting. Albi for me is one such dog. He does not have insurance cover and to my knowledge, it would have made no difference due to the fact that his health problems began from his start in Spain, before he even came to me as a foster dog. He has tested me and my bank balance to the limit but I would not change anything as what he has given me in return is priceless. Albi is like a bright sunny day.

Animals are all individuals and can have worries and anxieties that make their care a bit more problematic at times.

Milly is a worrier. If she is not sure about a situation, then she will go into reverse and try to get away; going to the vet has that effect on her. Fortunately, she has always been a healthy dog but the few times that she has had anaesthetic there is a plan in place so as to cause her as little upset as possible. Milly and I arrive early at the practice, the vet comes out to see her and gives the sedation, I stay with her until she is asleep, and then she is carried into the building. After surgery when the wound has healed, she will have the sutures removed in the van. I really appreciate the understanding of the staff to go to this effort for her.

Pippa and Marcus would get their acupuncture side by side in the back of the van, not because they were frightened but were so comfy in their beds leaving the vet and I to sit beside them catching up on chat.

Due to Tabitha dying on the operating table, whenever one of my dogs is having an anaesthetic a member of staff phones me as soon as they are awake. This is very thoughtful as I always worry; if it has happened once, could it happen again?

I believe it is about working together. By making a patient calm and a client happy, hopefully, the day is easier for a busy vet.

Chapter 15
Working with
Veterinary Students

An unexpected turn in Albi's story was when he was referred for specialist care. During his time as an inpatient, I spotted a poster at the hospital reception, asking for volunteers to participate in a programme working with veterinary students in the area of communication. I phoned the contact number and have been a member of this group since 2019. This work is part of their curriculum and the intention is to give the students time to spend with real clients, sharing, learning and listening to different experiences, outcomes and the effect that they have on clients. We enact role play using real-life documented scenarios.

I enjoy these sessions, there is fun, enthusiasm and you never know what questions will be asked and in what direction the conversation will go, but the best bit for me is when Albi and I get to do the meet-and-greet sessions together. It is a small part of the overall communication work, but so enjoyable. The students have 15 minutes with us and in that time, it is their job to find out as much as they can about Albi. Speed dating with dogs.

I have found over time that sitting on the floor with Albi and inviting the group to join us seems to be quite a good icebreaker, as we are all on the same level. There was one session where Albi worked his way around the students by reversing onto each person's knee and then giving them his undivided attention but he knew that we had limited time so he kept moving on without me having to ask. Another time, he did not seem to be concentrating and was wandering about, even standing at the door at one point. During the group changeover, I suggested that he should be making a bit more effort to join in. I was surprised; he had never acted like this before. When the second group came in, he did give us his full attention. The next time I spoke to Sarah-Jane I mentioned his behaviour and she reminded me that at that point she had been doing some long-distance energy work on him. Poor Albi, he is just like the rest of us, he cannot be in two places at once. Since that day, I always make sure that student work and Sarah-Jane's energy work are not double booked.

The big room we use for the pet sessions has lots of pieces of equipment to give the students the opportunity to familiarise themselves and have the time to practise how to use them. On another visit, Albi took a liking to a large cheetah soft toy, which was attached to an intravenous drip. After giving it a long sniff, he thought he might like to take it home, and had to be persuaded this was not a good idea. Everyone who knows Albi understands that in his heart there is a special place for large teddies.

At the end of each session, heading out into the corridor and down the staircase people call, 'Hi Albi' or, 'Bye Albi'. Despite the fact that he is deaf, he knows they are speaking to him and he looks so happy. Then we are through the doors and outside.

Albi has left the building!

Speaking to Sarah-Jane later he told her, "I am a star," and anybody watching him exiting the building certainly could get the impression that he is correct.

Life can be very strange with the twists and turns that it takes. Albi and I went to the referral hospital at a very difficult time when he was so unwell and yet ultimately it has led to such a positive outcome for his health and to our involvement in the Volunteer Programme, something that I would possibly otherwise never have been aware of.

Chapter 16
Slipping Away Peacefully

Albi has already shared with us that he is a Transition Dog. My own experience though, mostly with dogs and cats, has taught me the importance of the time of transition and death. Being part of the Volunteer Programme has given me the opportunity, along with others, to work with students, spending time sharing and discussing how deeply the loss of a greatly loved animal companion can be, and the importance of being able to help, comfort and support the client and their animal companion through the transition period passing from life to death.

To say goodbye to a loved animal companion is something every owner has to do at some point. This is the hard part of animal ownership and possibly the most important thing to get right. When working at the vet, I remember a situation that has stayed with me. One day, a client rushed past me on the way out the door. I was to find that her dog had been left to be put to sleep. This dog had been a lovely old family pet and this was now it's time. I remember sitting on the floor with the dog, talking to it and gently stroking its head. The needle was inserted by the vet, and the drug in the syringe was slowly released. With this, the dog peacefully went off to sleep. While comforting this animal, I felt such sadness for the dog that its owner was not there beside it sharing the final moments of life. A few months later, while out and about, I met the dog's owner who told me that she could not face being there at the end. I have always wondered at the time of booking the appointment for euthanasia whether one of the vets had spoken to the client and maybe asked what her fears were, and with discussion and questions answered that person may have felt it was possible to have been there. The dog and owner could have been a comfort to each other.

There is only one thing worse than losing a cherished companion and that is losing two pets close together. This brings double the distress and has happened to me on three occasions. I have already mentioned the deaths of Ricky and Tabitha a few weeks apart, followed by Marcus and Henry. Before that, there was Sophie and Bess who, along with Max, were our first sighthounds. Magnificent Max, I referred to previously, Sophie, a glorious and funny Whippet/Saluki cross, who was always known as Princess Sophie, and Bess, my first Greyhound, a sweet-natured dog who led me into the world of Greyhounds.

Two years after the charity was formed, Sophie had to be put to sleep due to a degenerative back problem and five days later, Bess was put to sleep because of an inoperable tumour. I can still remember the shock of that week. Having already written about putting to sleep Pippa, Marcus and Henry with Albi beside us, I am fortunate to have him now in my life as he made their passing a different experience.

I have found that if the procedure of putting to sleep is calm and peaceful, when the animal slips away it is a great comfort to the owner and they can be left feeling that they did the right thing at the right time. If the procedure does not go well for whatever reason, on top of the distress and sadness already felt, guilt and misery at their pet's final minutes can stay with an owner forever. Over the years, I have shared my life and my home with lots of wonderful dogs and cats. Also, working at a veterinary practice, I have seen different situations with animals being put to sleep either there or in a client's home. On many other occasions, I have been invited by the family to visit, for a final goodbye before one of my Gracehound's foster dogs was put to sleep or asked to be present at the time of putting to sleep. I am always very touched when at such a sad time, people remember me and take the time to make contact; it is so kind because I have never forgotten any of the dogs that have lived in my house before going on to their forever homes.

Over the years, I have worked out what is the best way for me to say goodbye to my animals but it is not always easy to have the discussion or know the questions to ask the vet. It can be helpful to have the conversation in advance if someone knows that their animal is nearing the end of its life. A chance to talk about the options, such as where will the animal be put to sleep, at home or at the veterinary practice. There are some practices that do not provide this service at home. How will it be carried out? What happens? Can the whole family be there? Can another family pet be present? Will my pet suffer? It is best if all questions are asked beforehand because if the situation changes and the animal has to be put to sleep quickly, without any time for discussion, important questions may be missed which can leave the owner with regrets.

There is also the question of cost. Again, there are different options and discussing money and bills at the time of putting a beloved pet to sleep can appear insensitive to a client and some vets also find it a difficult topic to raise. With options come costs which vary and for some people, there will be financial constraints that could mean what someone may like to do is different to what they can afford. Is it possible to pay the bill over weeks or months? The discussion around euthanasia is complex but it is so important to get it right for each owner and their pet.

I have mentioned being given the opportunity to say goodbye to some of my foster dogs and how grateful I am to be included at the end of life. During the time of Covid, I received phone calls from three families. The owners of two Spanish Galgos were the first. These dogs had travelled from Spain and arrived as my foster dogs. This had been organised by my paramedic friend, Pauline, who would later bring Milly and Albi into my life. They found their forever homes with families who had already adopted Greyhounds from me. Galgos look like Greyhounds but are slightly more comical as their noses can appear much longer. Now these lovely girls were old ladies having enjoyed long, happy lives.

I was invited to visit Abby at her home. She was a beautiful dog with striking markings, white with grey specs. Abby had arrived from Spain with a long-term health problem that would require monitoring all her life which certainly adds to the vet bills. Her family fell in love with her on their first meeting and they went on to do whatever was needed to keep Abby well and healthy for the remainder of her life. As always, she gave a wonderful welcome to us both, as Albi had come with me. Then, sitting down, she got stuck into her treats. I have never known a dog eat with such enthusiasm, maybe she had never forgotten her time living on the streets. To be able to talk and share the joy that she had given her family, for one last time, was a privilege.

The second call came from the other Galgo's mum asking if she could bring Niamh to visit me. This was arranged. Niamh walked through the gate and checked out the sofa that she had always enjoyed sitting on; it's on our verandah and she would spend hours there, soaking up the sunshine. She had such fun exploring the garden that afternoon and we spent some time just sitting with her, chatting. When Niamh had been with me, I always called her the duchess due to the fact that whenever we got ready for a walk she just stood at the back door of the van and waited for me to pick her up. She would stand still, like a statue, and that's how I lifted her up and put her in the van, position unchanged. It always made everybody laugh. What made her do this with me and nobody else is knowing the joy that dogs can have different relationships with each other and people just like humans can. When she went to her new home, she jumped into their car straightaway herself so nobody ever picked her up. Her mum and I reminisced about this funny routine. When it was time to leave, I walked with them down the drive and out to their car in the street. Then, the car door was opened and Niamh just stood. I bent down and picked her up from her standing position and lifted her into the car still standing, just like we had always done. Her mum and I looked at each other, we could not believe what we had just seen. It had been eight years since Niamh had left me but amazingly, she still remembered our little ritual which had obviously meant as much to her as it did to me. So sad to have to say goodbye but what a wonderful last few moments together.

The last story that I would like to share here is about Ewan. This large Brindle Greyhound was to be with me for six months as nobody was coming forward to show any interest in him. He was stunning to look at and had a lovely nature to match. One of the volunteer walkers had a soft spot for him and when he was with us on his weekly walk, he was always quick to take Ewan's lead. This family did not have a dog because they thought that work commitments made dog owning not practical. On his first day back walking after their summer holiday, he was very upset to find that there was still no home for Ewan. That evening a family meeting was called. Could they make it possible for Ewan to become part of their family? Everybody felt that they were prepared to do whatever was needed. That is how Ewan found his forever home and he enjoyed the best life for many years.

Eventually, the call came, it was now time to put Ewan to sleep, but the family were putting off making the final decision because of the lockdown due to Covid. They could not bear the thought of taking him to the vet as he was such a big dog and having to lift him in and out of the car would cause him distress. Also, they did not know if they would be able to be with him. When I went to see them, this lovely old dog got up on his wobbly legs to welcome me. Sitting beside him it was obvious that it was now his time but what to do for the best? As they were registered at the same veterinary practice as me it was agreed that I would make a call on their behalf to discuss the situation. I spoke to one of the vets that I knew well and she kindly said that it would be possible for her to come to the garden and Ewan could be put to sleep outside with his family beside him. Then, phoning the family, I relayed our conversation and would they now like to speak to the named vet to make arrangements. A few days later, I received a call from Ewan's family to say that all had gone well, he had slipped away with his family around him, which had given them all great comfort. I am aware that many people were not able to be with family during Covid either in hospitals or care homes, and many people had no choice but to hand their pets over at the vet's door, but this one family got their wish.

I did ask these three families if I could tell the stories of their pets' final days and may I use their names. To me, that was very important as the dogs' names were part of them. They all wanted Abby, Niamh and Ewan to be part of Albi's story.

Thank you.

Princess Sophie – Colin Sinclair

Max and Bess – Colin Sinclair

Abby and Lois – Lindsay Wright

Niamh in her favourite position on the verandah
– Lois Sinclair

Ewan – Colin Sinclair

Chapter 17
A Dog Called Alice

I had such high hopes for Alice.

I hoped she would be the right dog for our circumstances. I hoped that a warm friendship would develop between Albi, Milly and Alice. I hoped to introduce her to the benefits of puppy training and guide her through all the developmental stages that are needed to have a happy healthy well-balanced dog. Most of all, I hoped to provide her with a stable upbringing in her forever home.

Were my dreams fulfilled?

Yes! Alice has been everything I had hoped for and more. The three dogs bonded from the moment they met, the friendship between Milly and Alice is very strong, they take such delight in being together. Milly is going to be ten soon and is starting to slow down on walks so there are days when Alice is walked by herself as she needs to GO, GO, GO. And what a wonderful sight she is. On those days, Albi and Milly are walked at a gentler pace. He is a serial sniffer and as Milly likes to walk close to me and dawdles, they make a perfect pair.

I have worked hard on Alice's recall. Like many sighthounds, she has a strong prey drive so it is important that these dogs return when called. She is also restricted to where she gets off the lead. Alice has a best friend called Duke, a large, handsome Lurcher with no recall whatsoever. Wisely, he is not allowed the same freedom. Over time a group of us have got together and hired a large enclosed space once a week so that our eight sighthounds can enjoy the freedom of running off lead, and can build up to their top speed. It is a wonderful sight to see.

Alice loves life and all the people in it, including children and all dogs. Unfortunately, however, she has an unhealthy interest in squirrels and cats, so they are to be avoided at all costs. This dog is a brilliant ambassador for Greyhounds as she does not fit the classic look of many rescued Greyhounds. She does not walk slowly, with her head down, unable to play, and is wary of meeting new people. Newly rehomed Greyhounds, having had limited life experience of situations outside of racing kennels, are often afraid of other dogs or anxious about life in general. Alice has none of these concerns. We are often stopped by people who just want to check that she is a Greyhound because her whole demeanour is a bit different, there is just such joy about her. Adorned with a black, shiny coat, she is not huge but she is powerful with long skinny legs and muscles in all the right places. Last but not least, Alice has bucketloads of confidence; she must have been first in the queue when this was being handed out.

During the first lockdown, I considered taking in another dog if I heard about a Whippet needing a home. This did not happen but just in case it did, I asked Sarah-Jane to speak with Milly, Albi and Alice about my idea to see what they thought about it. Their replies sum up each dog perfectly.

Milly: "Not too young." If possible, she would like to have a say. "Mum, please do not take on too much. Little Pipsqueak, (Alice to you and I) is barely out of training pants."

Albi: "Whoopee! Another playmate to race around with." He also added, "Mum and Dad opened their hearts to us, so they should share what they have with another dog."

Alice: "Another playmate. Okay, but it is not allowed to be cuter than me!" That is our Alice.

Alice coming into our lives – Lois Sinclair

Chapter 18
A Lazy Summer Afternoon

For me, life has been fascinating, at times magical, exciting, sometimes sad, often funny and altogether amazing over the last few years thanks to the ups, downs and sheer joy that animals have brought into my life.

I asked Sarah-Jane if she would like to come and spend an afternoon with me, Albi, Milly and Alice in my favourite spot in the garden, beside the summerhouse surrounded by all the different grasses, of varying heights, which give such a lovely sound when there is a breeze. My special place indeed.

I asked Sarah-Jane to ask Milly how she was feeling now because I felt that she was slowing down on walks, which is why I had changed her to walk with Albi several days a week instead of Alice. Milly told Sarah-Jane that she likes going on shorter walks and she had taken to sitting down to have a scratch several times while we are out to allow herself to rest. I had noticed and guessed as much. She also told Sarah-Jane, "She and I are no longer spring chickens and I must be careful to not take on too much." Thanks, Milly, that makes me feel old and wrinkly.

Albi shared with Sarah-Jane that he now feels well and does not need to swim anymore for his rehabilitation, he just wants to enjoy his time in the water and likes all the attention that he is given by Pauline and Darryl. I am happy to drive over to Fife for a swim if everybody enjoys the outing. To see the big healthy, woolly bear of a dog that Albi has become is wonderful; the long haul and trauma to get here feels like a lifetime ago now.

What about Alice? She told Sarah-Jane that she loves the water but as she was speaking, Sarah-Jane said she had a strong sense of a lot of splashing and commotion going on, as if this beautifully graceful girl was anything but graceful in the water. I assured her that was quite correct. When swimming, Albi is calm and beautiful to watch. On the other hand, Alice clatters along making a huge amount of noise, having a whale of a time but not creating the image of a creature of beauty. This description of Alice is in complete contrast to her image on land where she is poetry in motion, elegant and fast. People do stop to watch her. Sarah-Jane shared that Alice does think she is beautiful, graceful and to be admired. She admitted to Sarah-Jane that she is high maintenance and loves being special. Sarah-Jane summed up Alice's feelings, needs and desires thus: "When she goes out, she is on show, has celebrity status and has to look her best." So, there you are, we have a celebrity in our midst!

Milly informed Sarah-Jane that she is kept busy looking after 'Pipsqueak' as nobody else keeps her in order. I found this strange because I always called Pippa by that nickname and here was Milly using the same name for Alice. I asked Sarah-Jane to ask Milly how she was because I knew that she missed her old companions. Who had been her special friend? Milly said, "I loved Marcus but Pippa was my friend." We are, of course, already aware of the similarities between Pippa and Alice. As she was speaking to me, Sarah-Jane remembered being aware of incredibly strong maternal feelings from Milly to Alice and knew that this was not the first time that these two had met; she just knew that they had been together before this lifetime. This gave both Sarah-Jane and I goosebumps. Alice had the same markings as Pippa. They were both feisty, brave, friendly and loving. Strangely, when Alice arrived, she appeared a bit lame on one of her back legs. We had assumed that it had been positioning on the journey, maybe how she had been lying, which had resolved itself after a few days. But this was the same leg that was missing on Pippa! Milly had been sad for so long. Is it possible that Pippa had come back to support Milly? We have already been told that Albi has been here before and he is back as he has work to do. Perhaps Pippa has, too. I will leave the reader to decide.

Then it was time to discuss with Albi a particular behaviour-related issue of his that was concerning me. What was the problem with Collies? He had begun to react to them and on occasion even lunged. Sarah-Jane took time to listen to Albi and understand things from his perspective. Albi said that he felt ashamed by his behaviour. He shared with Sarah-Jane that when he is on his lead and they are running free, the whoosh as they run back and forth is unsettling and made worse by the fact that he is deaf. There also seems to have been a situation where he had been nipped by a Collie, possibly by accident but the fear of it happening again worried him. So, what were we to do and how could I help? Sarah-Jane explained to Albi that whilst she understood his reaction, this behaviour could get us both into trouble and she asked him if he was open to working out a solution. We discussed a plan that he would be happy with. When a Collie runs towards us, he is to walk behind me and I will protect him. There is to be no lunging. Albi suggested a reward immediately for sticking to the plan: a sausage. Since Sarah-Jane and Albi's conversation, I am happy to report that walks have been brilliant. Albi and I keep to our plan, he seems calmer, there have been no more incidents and a steady stream of sausages are dispensed with.

This was then followed by the subject of Alice and her great interest in the world of squirrels. To date, it has amounted to just looking. When I suggested that she try to avert her gaze she gave Sarah-Jane a very determined, 'No'. She shared with Sarah-Jane that catching a squirrel is her dream, it would mean that she is at the pinnacle of her ability as a hunting sighthound. So, she and I are never going to agree in this area of animal welfare.

The conversation goes back and forth between us, with me asking questions and Sarah-Jane working directly with the dogs. It is so interesting to watch the dynamics of the dogs because one might presume that Albi is the boss yet he most certainly is not, nor has he any interest to be. It is Milly who steps forward and is given huge respect from Albi and Alice. We watch Albi standing at the door of the summerhouse wanting to come in but he would have to climb over Milly and he does not think that would be a good idea. After watching his predicament for a moment, I step in and guide him around her. The big brave boy said, "Thanks, Mum."

Anybody would be correct in thinking that Alice can be stroppy, there is a lot of noisy nonsense going on between Alice and Albi, in fact, it can become quite deafening. Albi, of course, is oblivious to sound, but we are not. Now Alice is starting to mimic some of his behaviour, such as not queuing up at the back door to get her harness and lead on but preferring to walk to the gate and get dressed there to go out. Retrieving balls is not an Albi thing which Alice enjoys but picking up a teddy and racing after Albi and his teddy, she is obviously copying the fun that he has. The enjoyment of having more than one dog at a time is how they interact as a group and their relationship. Three might be an odd number but in this case, Alice has benefited from having Albi and Milly to teach her. She has definitely cemented this happy band of dogs together.

As Albi has previously told us and he speaks for himself and Milly, "Alice is crackers but we love her." You get such a strong sense of this if you spend any time in their company.

Looking around at this little group, my eyes rest on Albi, this extraordinary dog, who gives so much to me and everybody that he comes into contact with. He is here to do a job, my Transition Dog, and of that I am in no doubt. He may one day have to leave us if he is called to be somewhere else. I have seen him suffer terrible pain in a dignified, quiet and stoical way. I have watched him bring peace, calm and comfort to the situation when Pippa, Marcus and Henry were each being put to sleep. I have watched him support friends when they have been distressed, just quietly coming in to be close and settle down beside them. He is here for Colin, my husband, who, with his progressive neurological condition, has not been able to enjoy walking his dogs for the last three years. Colin loves having Albi around, there is a bond and joy in their companionship.

I am blessed to have Albi in my life, he has been my teacher; from the moment he arrived six years ago, it was all meant to be. I have learnt about acceptance and living with what cannot be changed, love, compassion and generosity of spirit from this wonderful dog of mine.

Now, what of Milly and Alice? They are Albi's best friends; they give him love and joy. He is naughty and playful with them, just a dog having fun. I enjoy watching the three of them interacting together, whether running, chasing each other or just lying in a heap together and sleeping in the back of my van, it is Albi's time to be off duty. All this and more, that is why I called my book, *Learning from Albi*. Then, looking at Sarah-Jane, I think about what I have learned and experienced in a relatively short period of time. She has become my mentor and friend, sharing with me her world of animal communication, while encouraging and believing that I have my way of communicating with animals. She has helped me to understand that being in the company of animals is how I wish to live my life and to be able to help wherever I can.

It has been a wonderful afternoon.

So, thank you to Albi, Milly and Alice. You all bring me joy.

And, thank you Sarah-Jane Le Blanc for coming into my life.

Milly – Mihaela Bodlovic

Alice – Mihaela Bodlovic

Albi – Mihaela Bodlovic

Sarah-Jane and Lois with Albi, Milly and Alice – Derek Le Blanc

Chapter 19
From Patient to Film Star

The third week of March 2022 would prove to be unforgettable, with a strange turn of events, from the beginning through to the end of that week. It felt as though I was on a roller-coaster. This is how it began. I awoke on a Sunday morning and realised that Albi did not appear to be himself. He followed me into the bathroom and seemed not to know whether he wanted to stand, sit or lie down on the floor. He then had trouble getting up again onto his feet. I had to help him out of the bathroom and, once back in my bedroom, when I opened the wardrobe door, he climbed in. This had never happened before and I could not believe what I was seeing. Albi appeared at times not to understand what I was saying and he looked distressed, continually licking his lips, and at times had a vacant look in his eyes. He also had no appetite for breakfast. All in all, very odd behaviour. What was going on with him? I knew that he was trying to tell me something but I was completely baffled. I contacted the vet to arrange an appointment for the next day.

The following morning, Albi repeated the same routine, confirming that I had not imagined this unusual behaviour. While in the van waiting to go into the building, Albi rolled over and went to sleep. It looked a bit odd but he was to do this again in the consulting room in front of the vet, while I was explaining to her what had been going on. Fortunately, she knew Albi and I so well, as my story was such a strange mixture of events and symptoms. Albi continued to behave oddly in the consulting room culminating in reversing onto her knee when we were sitting on the floor with him. His mood was also extremely variable ranging from over-exuberance to low mood.

Albi's health has taken quite a prominent role in his extraordinary story so it was decided to put him through a complete health check with some routine bloods and other tests to make sure that everything was in order. The results all came back normal and he was given a clean bill of health. What next? I was pleased that physically he was fine, but I still knew he was trying to get my attention and that something was causing him concern. I contacted Sarah-Jane and asked her if I could bring Albi with me when we were planning to meet that Wednesday.

As we went into her house, Sarah-Jane could see immediately that Albi was not himself. Time to ask him what was going on. He described his head as being full and used the word 'overwhelmed' to explain the powerful sensation that he was experiencing. As I had suspected, Albi had been trying to get my attention. Sarah-Jane and I have learnt that Albi is not a worrier as he accepts what will be but he was concerned about Dad and his health issues. I realised that amongst the behaviours that Albi had been exhibiting, there were symptoms of Colin's health condition that were being mirrored. Colin, however, does not climb into wardrobes!

I have previously been told that animals can take on symptoms of health problems within their human family. Through Sarah-Jane, I could reassure him that it was not all his responsibility to take care of Dad but I did understand. This seemed to help him settle. Sarah-Jane voiced concerns about Albi's bad leg as she sensed there was a problem with it. It appeared to her that it needed a plaster cast or an old-fashioned splint that would support a broken femur if a human patient was in bed. We could not work this out and Albi did not elaborate any further. Did he have a premonition of what was to come?

Albi again shared with me through Sarah-Jane that Milly was worried about Dad and she was also feeling her age. It is hard getting older and keeping up with your best friend, Alice, who is only three.

When it came time to say goodbye, we left the house and all the odd behaviours that I had witnessed along with Sarah-Jane and the vet vanished never to be seen again. I could not believe the transformation. Albi had shared his concerns, had obviously been given the support he needed and felt reassured. Speaking to the vet later in the day, I said, "Hold onto your hat for what I am about to tell you!" Adding, I hoped she was sitting down while listening to my retelling of the conversation with Albi.

We were not going to be kept waiting long for the next Albi surprise or should I say shock.

Two days later in the evening after supper, with Milly and Alice in the house, Albi was found standing in the back garden by himself. The leg that had caused all the earlier problems was obviously broken, waving about, hanging from his body. He was standing on the steps trying to get himself up our sloping garden. On seeing him, I just knew that this leg was not going to be repairable, there had been too many problems. I was devastated, after all he had been through, we had come to this. My lovely boy, what was ahead for him now? With the help of two friends and a large towel, we managed to move him up the stone staircase and lift him into my van for the short trip to the vet.

By the time we arrived, Albi was in pain and appeared to be in shock, which was not surprising. He was given pain relief in the van before being carried into the practice. The first step involved taking X-rays to establish the extent of the damage and for the other legs to be checked for any potential problems. The X-rays showed that the fracture was spiral, and, as I had feared, likely to be irreparable. Fortunately, the joints on the other legs had no problems. This was important to know as it would inform the conversation that followed. The vet discussed the options with me. If there was no surgical intervention possible the question of whether to opt for amputation or euthanasia had to be considered.

Albi and I had gone this far together, there was no question in my mind of putting him to sleep now. However hard it is for vets to raise the subject, it was correct to do so, as how can decisions be made if all options are not addressed? The vet who had spent so much time caring for Albi over the previous four years was informed that he had been admitted and even though it was Friday evening and her weekend off, she took over his care. Everybody that night and over the next few days were fantastic, I knew that Albi was well looked after but it meant so much to me that she took the time to see him through yet another traumatic event.

It was agreed that Albi should be sedated overnight and the final decision was to be taken the following day. Everybody felt the only course of action was to amputate but one more phone call was to be made in the morning, to get in contact with the vet who had managed to remove the last pin from Albi's leg. Would he think it worth trying to save the leg or go straight to removal? It is always a good idea to discuss and share expertise, this gives support when making difficult choices.

The next morning with everybody concerned in agreement, it was time to amputate Albi's leg. I asked if I could go in and see him because I wanted to tell him myself what was going to happen. This done, I sat with him while the pre-med was given and he slipped off to sleep. Once he was about to be taken through to the operating theatre, I left and went home to wait.

Due to the fact that Albi's femur was brittle in places and not a healthy bone it was decided to remove the whole femur just in case there was any active infection still there but this made for a long operation. Compared with the surgery four years previously, when Albi had been an unwell dog, this time he was healthy and I knew that would make a difference to his recovery. A combination of an excellent vet, a supportive team and one very stoic dog, ensured that the whole procedure went without a hitch.

When I went to visit the following morning, Albi saw me coming through the door and got up on his three remaining legs. Once a member of staff opened the kennel door, he was through it and walking towards me.

It was a wonderful moment and his recovery went on from there; within two days he was home. There was only one tricky problem and that was the difficulty in urinating. To spare his blushes we do not need to go into too much detail but due to much swelling and bruising, I realised that he had always urinated standing on his bad leg. It was going to take a few days for him to get the hang of things such as balance and standing on the other back leg. But Albi is an adaptable dog and managed to overcome the problem quite quickly.

A month after last seeing Sarah-Jane, we were invited to be part of some filming that was taking place. A student who had spent the last four years making animal documentaries was now at Edinburgh University doing her Master's Degree in Filmmaking. She wanted to explore the world of animal communication and had approached Sarah-Jane. Several weeks of filming had already taken place with Sarah-Jane explaining how she worked. For our session, there was no forward planning, no discussion about what would be said or what topics would be raised. Whatever part of the filming that would be used for her documentary was what Albi would share with Sarah-Jane that afternoon.

At one point, Sarah-Jane saw a picture of a plaster cast again, but no leg, so she spoke to Albi about this strange vision. This time he did say that he would need some ongoing support but it was to be in the form of rehabilitation. He was happy to be told that he would be heading back to physiotherapy at the referral hospital where he had been treated for three months before the leg broke. He was also pleased to hear that we would be going back to Doggie Paddles in Fife for swimming. This would be for fun and he could enjoy taking the weight off the remaining three legs. He then asked me, through Sarah-Jane, if I would say a personal thank you to his vet from him, adding that everybody had been great but there was something special about his relationship with her. Sarah-Jane was overcome by how powerful this request felt and it made her tearful. I, however, was not surprised. I already knew.

A few days later, having read a copy of Albi's first book, the same student got in touch with me to say that she had been moved by his story and wondered if she could come to the house to film Albi at home and include his two special friends, Milly and Alice. This was organised for the following Sunday; she also asked if she could bring a friend along to help with the filming. It turned out to be a beautiful afternoon and all filming was done in the garden. Three hours later, with filming complete, it was time for the students to leave. Before they were even through the gate Albi was lying flat out, already sound asleep. Well, let's face it, being a film star is exhausting.

It has now been quite some time since Albi lost his leg. He is doing well and looks fabulous, there is a sparkle in his eyes and his thick, white coat is glossy. The big difference is how he appears in himself, extra joyful, as if a huge weight has been lifted, and to watch him run is incredible as his body shows no difficulty in coping with speed. He looks light on his remaining three legs.

This fits well with what his physiotherapist at the referral hospital says. She and Albi have worked hard together and the difference between what was possible to do with him before the fracture and the freer, easier and lightness in movements now is a transformation. His body, particularly his back, has lost all the tightness and tension that it had previously been carrying. Albi was having to work so hard to compensate for his bad leg and the pain that he was experiencing. Many thanks to Albi's physiotherapist who has played a huge part in his rehabilitation. Prior to each operation – there have been five in all – the hair on his back and damaged leg was shaved off, which always showed the skin to be red and hot to the touch. This time as the hair slowly returned, I saw a wonderful change that must show that Albi is finally, this time, on the mend. The skin on his back has changed from red to white and now feels cool to the touch. What would appear to have been constant inflammation has finally settled.

Albi resting at home after his amputation
– Lois Sinclair

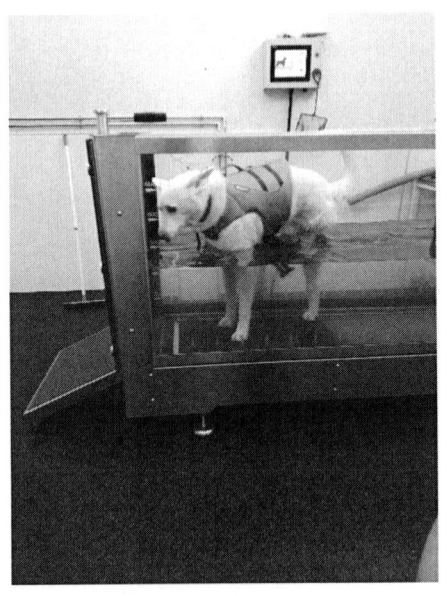

Albi attending the referral hospital for his physiotherapy
– Lois Sinclair

Chapter 20
Did I Mention Donkeys,
Goats and Ponies?

Having enjoyed the company of animals and being outside with nature all my life, I now realise that Albi's arrival did not put me on a different road but richly enhanced what was already there. He has created something deeper which I would like to spend the rest of my life exploring: the world of animal communication, with my own and other animals.

In the late summer of 2020, I found my way to a farm up in the hills not far from where I live, standing looking out over the amazing views which give such a sense of space, peace and being able to breathe deeply. The farm has the effect of drawing in people of all ages, people with years of riding experience and the inexperienced who are keen to learn. As well as horses, there are sheep and pigmy goats. Everyone has to spend time looking after the animals, in the morning and evening.

I enjoy feeding the goats and cleaning out their house, they are more my size, as they stand and watch you with their big marble eyes and for what appears to be no reason at all suddenly, butt you with those large horns. I have, over time, also noticed that during the winter they hang about their hut area a little cross and stroppy, then out comes the sun and warm days and, just like humans, they become calmer and more biddable while moving about the fields.

There are five goats and I find it hard to tell the boys apart due to their colouring but the two girls look different. They each like attention but the one that was the smallest when they arrived as kids a few years ago, is the most affectionate. Her name is Tallulah. One day, while spending time with them, I noticed that she was just sitting quietly by herself so I sat down beside her. It was not long before she relaxed, enjoying a stroke, with her eyes closing in delight and her breathing changing to a gentle slow pace. What a lovely way to start the day, sitting in the sunshine and giving a little goat a cuddle.

Then there are the horses, which to me appear huge and beautiful. I enjoy learning about them but have absolutely no desire to ride at all, ever, though I would like to be more confident around them, and to feel that I know what I am doing, but that may take a long time. There is one person there who, when she sees me looking anxious, thinks that it is helpful to shout, "Just pretend it's a large dog." That will never work!

There is a little pony that I am particularly fond of, whose name is Ollie, he is quite feisty and can be challenging to work with, way beyond my ability but one game that gives him pleasure is hunting the treat in a scrunched-up tea towel. I have had some lovely times when he comes up and nestles his head into me. We have a quiet chat and then just like Tallulah, his eyes close and the sound of his breathing changes. These are special moments.

I had not been at the farm long when it was mentioned that there were two donkeys down the road living on a small holding. That day when finishing at the farm, I went straight to introduce myself to the donkeys and their owner. That is how Seamus, Hattie and their horse companion, Bertie, came into my life.

Donkeys are such special animals, and these two are important to me. I spend time with them grooming, playing games and doing pole work. A lot of hugging goes on. Seamus likes to rest his head on my back or will wrap a front leg around one of mine to get attention. Going for a walk with a donkey is such a lovely thing to do, I think that it is the sound of clip-clopping along. They hear my van coming through the country lanes and run down the hill to welcome me. Of all animals, donkeys have the funniest run and with their big gentle eyes, you can see into their souls. I am often welcomed with a loud 'Hee Haw'. Seamus is the extrovert, who loves to be groomed, hanging his head over the gate and shutting his eyes with pleasure as the brush moves around his face and ears. Hattie, his sweet companion, is not so pushy but quietly enjoys any attention given to her.

Seamus was recently invited to attend the Easter Service at one of the local churches, so along with his owner, Jo, we walked him there, through the streets and to the church. It is extraordinary how people are drawn to donkeys. As we walked along, people crossed the road to join us, cars slowed down and waved, and people came out of shops. The wonder of donkeys. They have always had that effect on me but it is interesting to see other people's reactions. It was the same when I volunteered at the donkey sanctuary. When we showed visitors around, introducing them to the donkeys, adults and children alike were always enchanted to meet them close up.

The minister had not shared with his congregation that there would be a special visitor. On arriving at the church, Seamus walked up the front steps and through the door. We had no idea that the place would be full. Jo, his owner, led him down the main carpeted aisle, with me bringing up the rear clutching a packet of Seamus' favourite ginger snaps. The place was in uproar with people laughing, clapping and taking pictures. That was just the adults, the children's faces were filled with joy. The minister was waiting for us at the front of the church. This wonderful little donkey has a huge personality. If he was human, I think he would be called a party animal. He stood still, waiting to be introduced while the importance of the Easter donkey was explained. With that done, we were on our way back down the aisle and out the door. What fun that had been, watching a donkey spreading joy.

The farm and small holding are different, but both give me opportunities to learn about and build, relationships with other animals and I am well aware of what an important part they play in my life. So, thank you to the humans in both places who have kindly welcomed me in.

Lois with Tallulah – Kerry Stephan

Ollie and Lois – Kerry Stephan

Seamus and Lois – Jo Pagett

Seamus and Hattie – Lois Sinclair

Lois with Hattie and Seamus – Jo Pagett

Chapter 21
Time to Stop Worrying

Animals of all sorts, and my relationships with them, bring joy to my life but it is my time spent with dogs that has been particularly influential. It is only right then, that I should bring this particular story to a close by introducing you to my most recent canine arrival, Polly.

First of all, I should clarify, throughout *Learning from Albi,* there have been three Paulines mentioned: Pauline Shirlaw, my closest friend, Pauline at Doggie Paddles and finally Pauline, paramedic and dog rescuer extraordinaire, who works under the title of Forever Hounds. The latter, I first met when I still had Gracehounds and one of my dog walking volunteers was a friend of Pauline and asked her if she could visit me to discuss rescue work. Having had many holidays in Spain over the years, she had become aware of the plight of the hunting dogs and hoped to help some by bringing them over to Scotland for homing. So began the wonderful work that Pauline has done with such commitment for many years.

A few months ago, Pauline asked me if I could foster a little hound puppy that was still in the Perrera 'killing station'. She had chosen Polly because being black there would not be much hope of her getting adopted by anyone. This struck a chord with me because I know from past experience that black Greyhounds are harder to home. As soon as I said yes, Pauline began to put arrangements in place. I then asked Sarah-Jane to speak to Milly, explaining about our new arrival. Nothing goes quite to plan as my friend Pauline and I were going to be away for two nights at a hotel when the transport was scheduled to leave Spain and my dogs would be in kennels. Both Pauline and I are carers for our partners and we enjoy a break every few weeks. I am extremely fortunate to have a wonderful family and blessed with great friends who rally around to support Colin while I am away.

Thus, the conversation between Sarah-Jane and my dogs goes like this. Milly tells Sarah-Jane that she is very happy in the kennels. It is lovely for me to hear because many years ago, when all the dogs went into kennels together, Milly, who has been with me for nine years, would have to be carried in. And now? She leads the way, running! Sarah-Jane felt that Alice was nearby but not close. I told her in the feedback that is correct as she is in the next-door kennel. Milly shared with Albi and said that she likes that best because she cannot always cope with all the energy that she feels from Alice.

Milly said that she knew Polly was coming and she wants to help me with another dog, also it is fine if Polly is a foster or if she stays. Milly seems to finally believe that she is in her forever home and I can feel her newfound confidence.

Albi said that his broken leg was an accident waiting to happen, he is fine but does worry when with another dog, that his one remaining back leg may get knocked. Sarah-Jane reassured him that I would keep an extra special eye on him and he was happy with that and another dog is okay by him.

Alice…well, who would be surprised by what she says? "As long as she does not steal my limelight." Apparently, Milly stepped in to say that she would be able to reassure Alice. This feedback helped me believe that everything would work out.

On Wednesday morning at the hotel, the photos started coming through of Polly being put in the van in Spain. It was the first time I had seen her face and what a dear little face it was. We were shown around the air-conditioned transport and all the individual kennels with beds and water. We were told that they would be stopping at regular intervals and the dogs would be walked and photographed. This was about around ten in the morning and through WhatsApp, we were to be part of the journey until Polly arrived at my house. We could also track where they would be. When it was all over, I was exhausted having felt that I had been on the trip with them.

Pauline and I came home a little earlier so we could collect my dogs from kennels at teatime as I wanted them home for the arrival of Polly later on the Thursday night. I had been told the arrival time and on the dot of 11.30 pm, the van was at my gate. I picked her out of her crate. She was in perfect condition and came straight to me for a hug.

The next day, Pauline and Maria came to meet Polly. Pauline shared with me that Polly had a brother and sister still in the killing station and she was worried as she had been told that the hunting season was approaching and was afraid that they may be picked out by the hunters. This often does not have a good outcome, as hunting dogs can be handed back at the end of the season or killed so that they do not need to be fed over the winter. I told Pauline to get them out, we would manage and I can foster.

There was no holding Pauline back as, without hesitation, she contacted the fosterer in Spain, who confirmed that she could take them and arrangements were quickly put in place to collect Pepe and Sofia from the Perrera and take them to the foster carer. One month later, Pepe and Sofia would make the same journey as their sister had. They would both come to me for a couple of days. I wondered if I had maybe stretched myself a bit thinly so phoning my cousin, I asked her if she would be free for two days to give me an extra pair of helping hands. Luckily, she was. Two days before the pups arrived, Sarah-Jane spoke to my dogs to explain to them that we would have Polly's brother and sister arriving.

My cousin and I sat up all through the night waiting for the puppies to arrive. Finally, at 4.30 am the van drove into the garden. It had been a long journey for these two little souls. On carrying them into the house, there suddenly seemed to be puppies everywhere. It was extraordinary that Polly, Sofia and Pepe all instantly recognised each other and for me to see them all together again was wonderful. I was drawn to Pepe, I am not sure why but I think that he reminded me of Marcus. He was the biggest of the three and there was a gentleness about him. He certainly wanted to be picked up and hugged a lot. It was going to prove later to be hard to say goodbye to him. Sofia was the smallest and dainty little girl compared to her huge sister, Polly. All three had enormous appetites and upset tummies so a bucket and mop had to be standing at the ready to go into action when needed. Milly, Albi and Alice were incredibly calm. My cousin, who is a cat person, could not believe the mess and noise but it did not stop her from being a big help and after two days, she went home exhausted.

So, what happened to Polly, Sofia and Pepe? Polly and Alice bonded from the word go and it was not a difficult decision to keep her. She became Phoebe. Sofia became Sophie and Pepe would become Max. They would both go to families in Perthshire and it would help them heal after the grief of each losing a beloved dog. I asked the families if they would like to share what it has meant to them having Max and Sophie in their lives.

For Ian and Jill: Max is Ian's best pal and Jill says he brings joy and warmth with a lot of fun.

I have spoken about joy throughout this book, for me it is the essence of having a dog in my life and here was Jill using the same word.

What about Sophie's family? Karen wrote, "After losing our beautiful Collie dog in June 2022, our other dog Timmy was lonely and we had a heartbroken eight-year-old daughter. Then in August, I was taken into the hospital for an emergency operation. After a few months of misery and grief, my friend Jill asked if I would be interested in Max's sister Sofia. I instantly thought that this is what we all need. She was to be with me while I recovered. Sophie, our little heart healer."

Thanks to Pauline, Phoebe, Max and Sophie were found, taken to a place of safety and then on to their forever homes. For myself, Ian and Jill, Karen and her family what these three puppies have brought into our lives is joy.

What of my dogs and their new friend? Milly has been so kind and helpful; she has decided that she no longer wishes to sleep upstairs but sleeps in a dog bed beside Phoebe's crate. Albi kept his distance to start with and had beds all over the place but has now come back into the fold and is enjoying playing with Phoebe. I do as I promised and keep a close eye on him so that there is no chance of him being knocked over. What about Alice? Well, she has found her perfect playmate and they are having great fun together. She is suddenly looking older and more mature with a job to do. Phoebe loves sitting with Alice, then curling up beside her and going to sleep. So, what can I say? It was written in the stars.

Let us now go back to Albi whose story is coming to a close. The reader has learned about this extraordinary dog, other wonderful dogs and a very special cat. Then the reader was introduced to the joy of donkeys, horses and goats then finally back to the dogs, the arrival of Phoebe and her two siblings Sophie and Max.

But the last word has to be about Albi. It is now March 2023 and one year since his leg snapped in our garden and had to be amputated. It has been mentioned previously that during the recovery period, the red hot skin on Albi's back had changed to cool on touch and was no longer red in colour but white. There is one more change that I would like to share. Remember Albi's love of giant teddy bears? Well, over the last few months, something has happened. They seem to be no longer needed. I had wondered if they were for comfort during the time of all his pain then, not long ago, talking to a friend about this change she told me that when her son was little, he had had osteomyelitis and he had carried around a giant pillow for comfort. So maybe this is Albi saying now loud and clear that he is no longer in pain. The thought makes me very happy.

Recently, Albi said to Sarah-Jane that he was, "Now going to live his best life, and that Mum could stop worrying."

Albi is well, fit and happy. That is all that I ever wanted for him, my amazing Spanish Podenco.

What does the future hold for him and I? We will just have to wait and see.

Sofia and Pepe in the crate and Polly on the stool
– Lois Sinclair

Phoebe – Lois Sinclair

Albi living his best life – Lois Sinclair